Horatio R. Palmer

Palmer's Sabbath School Songs

To Which is Added an Extensive Collection of Standard and Well-Known...

Horatio R. Palmer

Palmer's Sabbath School Songs
To Which is Added an Extensive Collection of Standard and Well-Known...

ISBN/EAN: 9783337089603

Printed in Europe, USA, Canada, Australia, Japan

Cover: Foto ©Thomas Meinert / pixelio.de

More available books at **www.hansebooks.com**

Palmer's

Sabbath School Songs;

TO WHICH IS ADDED

AN EXTENSIVE COLLECTION

OF STANDARD AND WELL-KNOWN

SUNDAY SCHOOL HYMNS,

BY

H. R. Palmer,

*Author of "The Song Queen," "Rudimental Class Teaching," "Elements of
Musical Composition," Musical Editor of " The
Sunday School Teacher,"
Etc., Etc.*

CHICAGO:

Published by Adams, Blackmer, and Lyon,

No. 155 Randolph Street.

SUGGESTIONS

TO SUPERINTENDENTS AND CHORISTERS.

FOR the sake of convenience, the Hymns have been divided into classes: such as those for Sabbath Schools, Social Meetings, Temperance, Missionary, Funeral Occasions, etc. It was found impossible to conform strictly to this plan in arranging the music pages; but a glance at the title in the index will always suggest the class to which the piece belongs. The Hymns for social meetings have been selected with reference to the wants of Teachers' Meetings and family worship. Still they are, in every instance, words which the children *ought* to learn, and will be found very useful upon occasions when a deep spiritual interest is manifested in the school. In adapting the Hymns to tunes, we have referred to as many different books as practical, but the book and tune which is printed first *is our preference.*

By way of introduction, we would call attention to the following pieces: "Looking to Jesus;" "Angry Words;" "Beautiful Home;" "I will Seek my Father;" "Only Waiting;" "Little Pilgrim on the Road;" "Father Rock us;" "Children may Come to the Saviour;" "Loved Ones Gone Before;" "Singing from the Heart;" etc., etc.

With regard to "Tell Him to Halt!" we wish to say that, although it has been the subject of slight criticism, it has, nevertheless, attained a sudden and wide-spread popularity, and we insert it, deferring to the opinion of the people, rather than to that of the critic.

One of the greatest aids in keeping up good singing, is the *Sunday School Choir,* which should consist of eight or ten of the best singers in the school from eleven to fifteen years of age. The chorister should spend an hour or so, each week, in teaching the choir to sing new songs, thus enabling them to render very material aid when he wishes to introduce these songs to the school. After much experience in conducting Sabbath School music, the author has found that no feature awakens a more lively interest on the part of the members, than a special piece well sung by the choir each Sunday; more especially if the scholars are given to understand that they are to learn these new songs after a few Sabbaths. At first, the choir may consist of two members (a soprano and an alto), and may be augmented from time to time by the addition of any good singer who manifests a disposition to work.

While many of the pieces are written as solos, duets, etc., they are within the compass of all voices, and may be sung in unison *by the whole school* with great effect; indeed, they should usually be sung in this way.

The player will find that a piece of elastic cord, stretched around the book rack, will be very convenient in keeping the book open. Every page is complete in itself; hence there is no necessity for turning the leaves after the book is once in position.

We are under obligations to Messrs. Root & Cady, Messrs. Biglow & Main (successors to Mr. Bradbury), Messrs. F. J. Huntington & Co., Mr. J. M. North, Rev. R. Lowry, and others, who have kindly permitted us to reprint many valuable pieces from their publications. Also, to Dr. C. R. Blackall, Rob. Morris, LL.D., and many others (whose names appear over their respective pieces), for original hymns written expressly for this work.

NOTICE. — Both words and music are COPYRIGHT PROPERTY; those which are owned by others we print with especial permission; hence no one is at liberty to reprint them FOR ANY PURPOSE WHATEVER without first obtainingthe consent of the owners.

CHICAGO, *June,* 1868.   H. R. PALMER.

PALMER'S
SABBATH SCHOOL SONGS.

Children's Voices.

Inscribed to the Sunday School of the First Baptist Church.

Words by T. S. CHARD.　　　　　　　　　　　H. R. PALMER.

1. Chil - dren's voi - ces join'd in praise, Lov - ing an - gels wait to hear,
2. Chil - dren's voi - ces rais'd in prayer, Bring a bless-ing from a - bove,
3. Chil - dren's voi - ces gen - tle, kind, Ev - er used in ac - cents mild,
4. Chil - dren's voi - ces wail - ing low, Je - sus sym - pa - thiz - ing hears,

For the Sab - bath song they raise, Reaches the e - ter - nal ear.
For the Lord who reigneth there, Is a God whose name is love.
Shall a read - y list - 'ner find, Who Him - self was once a child.
He him - self has suf - fer'd so, And will gent - ly dry their tears.

Refrain. (Arr. from Sir. H. R. Bishop.)

Then let us now our voi - ces bring, And with our

Then let us now our voi - ces bring, And with our

Of Him who is our Lord and King.

hearts the glory sing, Of Him who is our Sav - ior, Lord and King.

hearts the glory sing, Of Him who is our Sav - ior, Lord and King.

Of Him who is our Lord and King.

I'll Away to Sabbath School.

S. S. BELL, No. 1—52, Key of B flat.

1. When the morning light drives away the
    night,
  With the sun so bright and full,
And it draws its line near the hour of nine,
  I'll away to the Sabbath School,
  For 'tis there we all agree,
  All with happy hearts and free,
  And I love to early be,
    At the Sabbath School :
  I'll away ! away ! I'll away ! away !
  I'll away to Sabbath School !

2. On the frosty dawn of a winter's morn,
  When the earth is wrapped in snow,
Or the summer breeze plays round the
    trees,
  To the Sabbath School I go.
    When the holy day has come,
    And the Sabbath breakers roam,
    I delight to leave my home,
    For the Sabbath School :
  I'll away, &c.

3. In the class I meet with the friends I
    greet,
  At the time of morning prayer ;
And our hearts we raise in a hymn of
    praise,
  For 'tis always pleasant there :
    In the Book of holy truth,
    Full of counsel and reproof,
    We behold the guide of youth,
    At the Sabbath School :
  I'll away, &c.

4. May the dews of grace fill the hallow'd
    place,
  And the sunshine never fail.
While each blooming rose which in mem-
    ory grows,
  Shall a sweet perfume exhale ;
    When we mingle here no more,
    But have met on Jordan's shore,
    We will talk of moments o'er,
    At the Sabbath School :
  I'll away, &c.

To-day !

Tune.---Chide mildly the erring, G. Chain 56,
    Key of D.

1. Watch closely the pathway
    God marks for thee here,
  Be ready to cherish,
    E'er willing to cheer ;
  Lift up by thy kindness,
    The low trodden down,
  ‖: Go weep with the mourners,
    And brotherhood own. :‖

2. Wait not for the future,
    Time's passing away,

Fill hours that are present,
    God calleth to-day !
  As leaves in the autumn,
    Lie strewn all around,
  ‖: So, means to be useful
    Do ever abound. :‖

3. Grow nearer to Jesus,
    Trust always his love,
  He kindly will lead you,
    His grace you may prove :
  Avoid what is sinful,
    And cleave to the true,
  ‖: Obeying the Saviour
    In all that you do. :‖

Dr. C. R. Blackall.

Sunday School Recruiting Song.

G. CHAIN, Key of A ; also S. S. Hosanna 66.

1. To our dear Sabbath School there
    ought many to come,
Who spend Sunday wandering or trifling
    at home ;
I'll try to bring *one*, or I'll try to bring *two*,
Yes, all that I can I'm determined to do.
God meant all the people who live in this
    place
To hear of his goodness and join in his
    praise ;
So I'll try to bring *one*, or I'll try to bring
    two,
Yes, all that I can I'm determined to do.

2. Let me think : are there none of the
    dear ones at home,
The large or the little, who never have
    come ?
Oh, I'll beg, and I'll coax, try for *one*, try
    for *two*,
Yes, all that I can I'm determined to do.
My cousins and playmates, who live in
    this street,
I'll ask them to come, the next time that
    we meet ;
Who knows but among them I'll get *one*
    or *two* ?
For all that I *can* I'm determined to do.

3. Out there in the lot that I pass every day,
How many spend Sunday in frolic or play !
If I could but get *one* of those boys, now,
    or *two*,
To come here next Sabbath, what good it
    might do !
Perhaps up to heaven some day I may go ;
What glory and blessedness then I shall
    know !
But I want in that glory that many may
    share,
That one, two, yes, all I can take, may be
    there.

Singing from the Heart.

Words by ROB. MORRIS, L L. D.

Music by H. R. PALMER.

1. If you have a pleas-ant thought, Sing it. Sing it, Like the bird-ies in their sport,
2. Every gracious deed of His, Sing it, Sing it, Nothing sounds so well as this,
3. Are you wea-ry are you sad ? Sing it, Sing it, Make yourselves and others glad,

Sing it from the heart, Does the ho - ly spirit move, For the lamb-kins of His love
Sing it from the heart. How he walked upon the wave,—Resened Laz'rus from the grave,
Sing it from the heart. An-gels up be-fore His face Sing of His redeeming grace;

Refrain.

Sing and point the fold above, Sing it from the heart. Singing, singing from the heart,
Died our guilty souls to save, Sing it from the heart.
Give the Savior endless praise, Sing it from the heart.

Sing-ing, singing from the heart,

Oh the joys our songs impart ! Je-sus bless the tune-ful art, Singing from the heart.

Oh the joys our songs impart ! Je-sus bless the tune-ful art, Singing from the heart.

Sabbath Welcome.

Tune.---"Union Greeting." (See opposite page.)

1. Best of the seven ! Oh, holy day,
That lights the track of our young life's
    way,
  The day of praise and prayer ;
We love the glory that marks thy morn,
We sing thy worth to the sad and worn,
  Oppressed by toil and care.
CHORUS.—Oh ! Cheerily, Cheerily, sing
    we the strain,
  Welcome thou Sabbath of rest !
Joyfully, Joyfully, welcome again,
  Sabbath, dear Sabbath of rest !
  Welcome ! Welcome !
  Welcome dear Sabbath of rest !

2. Turning from Earth's busy paths aside,
We join in songs of the ONE who died,
  But rose on this glad day ;
Our hearts keep time to the music clear,
Of Angels bright, in the heavenly sphere,
  That never shall pass away !
  CHO.—Oh ! Cheerily, &c.

3. Happy this day do we offerings bring,
And pure the songs that with joy we sing.
  To him who reigns above ;
We know that each in His love doth share,
We know that each hath his tender care
  That naught shall ever move.
  CHO.—Oh ! Cheerily, &c.
          Dr. C. R. Blackall.

The Morning Bells.

G. CHAIN 51, Key of A, S. S. Bell ; No. 1—50.

1. Hark ! the morning bells are ringing !
  Children, haste without delay ;
Prayers of thousands now are winging
  Up to heaven their silent way.
CHO.—Come, children, come ! the bells
    are ringing,
  To the school with haste repair ;
  Let us all unite in singing,
  All unite in solemn prayer.

2. 'Tis an hour of happy meeting,
  Children meet for praise and prayer ;
But the hour is short and fleeting,
  Let us then be early there.
  CHO.—Come, children, come ! &c.

3. Do not keep our teachers waiting,
  While you tarry by the way,
Nor disturb the school reciting :
  'Tis the holy Sabbath day.
  CHO.—Come, children, come ! &c.

4. Children, haste ! the bells are ringing,
  And the morning's bright and fair ;
Thousands now unite in singing,
  Thousands, too, in solemn prayer.
  CHO.—Come, children, come ! &c.

Forbid Them Not.

HAPPY VOICES 29 ; Key of B flat.

1. When many to the Saviour's feet
  Their little children brought,
And from the source of blessedness
  A Saviour's blessing sought ;
To some who with mistaken zeal
  The near approach forbade,
" Let little children come to me,"
  The blessed Saviour said.

2. " Forbid them not, nor harshly chide
  Their wish to see my face ;
For little children such as these
  My Father's kingdom grace."
Then, gather'd in his loving arms
  And folded to his breast,
He pour'd a blessing all divine
  On every little guest.

3. Dear children, Jesus is the same,
  Though now enthroned above ;
He waits to bless you, as of old,
  With his forgiving love.
He marks with joy each faint attempt
  His favor to obtain,
And those who early seek his face
  Shall never seek in vain.

4. But sin prevents, and Satan strives
  To keep you from his arms ;
And to allure the soul away,
  The world displays it charms.
But look to Jesus, for his power
  Your foes can ne'er withstand ;
Let him but say, " Forbid them not,"
  They'll fly at his command.

Come to the Sabbath School.

Tune—"There is a happy land ;" Key of E flat.

1. Come to the Sabbath School, all chil-
    dren come ;
Cheerful its pious rule, pleasant as home ;
Leave rude and naughty plays, love and
    keep the holy days,
Come, learn to pray and praise in Sab-
    bath School.

2. Come, where our teachers meet, faith-
    ful and true ;
Come, learn the lessons sweet, ready for
    you ;
Come, school will not be long ; come, and
    join our happy throng ;
Come, sing our pretty song in Sabbath
    School.

3. Oh, there's a school on high, where an-
    gels praise ;
Joy beams in every eye, sweet strains they
    raise ;
There seraph children sing anthems to
    our glorious King,
And crowns to Jesus bring,—blest Sab-
    bath School.

The Union Greeting.

Words by DR. BLACKALL.

Music by G. C. PEARSON.

1. Hith-er we come, as a Un-ion Band, To sing sweet songs of a bet-ter land,
2. Greeting we give on this fes-tive night, A hap-py lay of the heart's delight,
3. Gems have we brought to delight the soul, And flow'rs whose fragrance shall e'er be whole,

The land of peace and love; Where Je-sus reigns as a King a-lone,
Good will on ev-ery hand; Bright eyes are beam-ing a-mid the throng,
That cheer life's way a-long; Then give your hearts and ex-tend your hands.

And all His child-ren fond-ly own Their Fath-er, God a-bove,
And young hearts glow as they sing the song Of this our Un-ion band.
And let us bind you in silk-en bands, The bands of love and song.

Refrain.

Oh! mer-ri-ly, mer-ri-ly, joy-ous and free, Sing we the song of the

last stanza. Oh! joy-ous-ly, joy-ous-ly sound we the strain, For 'tis the song of the

true; Cheer-i-ly, Cheer-i-ly, hap-py are we, Warm is our welcome to

true, Cheer-i-ly, Cheer-i-ly give we a-gain, Welcome, thrice welcome t

Boys. Girls Together.

you. Welcome! Welcome! Warm is our wel-come to you!

you. Welcome! Welcome! Welcome, thrice welcome to you!

*From Chapel Gems, by Permission of Root & Cady.

Happy Greeting to All.

S. S. BELL, No. 1—17, Key of E flat; also Oriola 62, or G. Tidings 46.

1. Come, children, and join in our festival song,
And hail the sweet joys which this day brings along;
We'll join our glad voices in one hymn of praise
To God, who has kept us and lengthen'd our days.
CHORUS.—Happy greeting to all !
Happy greeting to all !
Happy greeting, happy greeting,
Happy greeting to all !

2. Our Father in heaven, we lift up to thee
Our voice of thanksgiving, our glad jubilee;
Oh, bless us, and guide us, dear Saviour, we pray,
That from thy blest precepts we never may stray.
CHORUS.—Happy greeting, &c.

3. And if, ere this glad year has drawn to a close,
Some loved one among us in death shall repose,
Grant, Lord, that the spirit in heaven may dwell,
In the bosom of Jesus, where all shall be well.
CHORUS.—Happy greeting, &c.

4. Kind teachers, we children would thank you this day
That faithfully, kindly, youv'e taught us the way
How we may escape from the world's sinful charms,
And find a safe refuge in the Saviour's loved arms.
CHORUS.—Happy greeting, &c.

5. Dear pastor, we ask thee, as lambs of thy fold,
To teach us that wisdom more precious than gold ;
Our footsteps to guide in the pathway of truth,
To "love our Creator in the days of our youth."
CHORUS.—Happy greeting, &c.

God Speed the Right.

OLIVE BRANCH 75, Key of D; also G. Chain 8.

1. Now to heaven our prayer ascending,
God speed the right !
In a noble cause contending,
God speed the right !
Be their zeal in heaven recorded
With success on earth rewarded.
God speed the right !
God speed the right !

2. Be that prayer again repeated,
God speed the right !
Ne'er despairing, though defeated,
God speed the right !
Like the good and great in story,
If they fail, they fail with glory.
God speed the right !
God speed the right !

3. Patient, firm, and persevering,
God speed the right !
Ne'er the event or danger fearing,
God speed the right !
Pains, nor toils, nor trials heeding,
And in heaven's own time succeeding,
God speed the right !
God speed the right !

4. Still their onward course pursuing,
God speed the right !
Every foe at length subduing,
God speed the right !
Truth, thy cause, whate'er delay it,
There's no power on earth can stay it.
God speed the right !
God speed the right !

Who Shall Sing ?

G. CHAIN 14. Key of G ; also S. S. Bell, No. 1—35

1. Who shall sing, if not the children ?
Did not Jesus die for them ?
May they not with other jewels,
Sparkle in his diadem ?
Why to them were voices given,
Bird-like voices, sweet and clear,
Why, unless the song of heaven
They begin to practice here ?

2. There's a choir of infant songsters,
White-robed, round the Saviour's throne ;
Angels cease, and, waiting, listen !
Oh, 'tis sweeter than their own !
Faith can hear the rapturous choral,
When her ear is upward turn'd ;
Is not this the same, perfected,
Which upon the earth they learn'd !

3. Jesus, when on earth sojourning,
Loved them with a wondrous love ;
And will he, to heaven returning,
Faithless to his blessing prove ?
Oh, they cannot sing too early !
Fathers, stand not in their way !
Birds do sing while day is breaking—
Tell me, then, why should not they ?

By and By.

Inscribed to Trinity Mission Sunday School.

H. R. PALMER.

1. We shall see the gol-den ci-ty, By and by, By and by, Walk the streets of the
2. Wea-ry hearts will be unburdened, By and by, By and by, Sore and sor-row-ful
3. Jesus says that we shall be with him, By and by, By and by, Live and reign in

gol-den ci-ty. Yes, by and by; We shall meet the beautiful an-gels,
hearts un-bur-dened, Yes, by and by! We shall part with all our trou-bles
Par-a-dise with him, Yes, by and by. We shall meet and sing for-ev-er,

By and by, By and by. Meet and sing with the beautiful angels, Yes, by and by.
By and by, By and by. Change the cross for a crown of glo-ry, Yes, by and by.
By and by, By and by. Sing the prais-es of God for-ev-er, Yes, by and by.

Refrain.

Join and march to that bet-ter coun-try, Seek the prize, the crown of glo-ry,

Join and march to that bet-ter coun-try, Seek the prize, the crown of glo-ry.

Cherish the hope of the home that waits thee, Yes, by and by

Cherish the hope of the home that waits thee, Yes, by and by.

We are Little Sunbeams.

CHAPEL GEMS 78, Key of G.

1. We are little sunbeams,
   Shining and free,
We are little sunbeams,
   Happy are we ;
No clouds our skies o'ercast,
   No storms are here,
Our brightness e'er shall last,
   We will not fear,
CHORUS.—We are little sunbeams,
   Shining and free,
   We are little sunbeams,
   Happy are we.

2. We are little sunbeams,
   Like those above,
We are little sunbeams,
   Warming with love.
Into dark haunts of woe,
   Sorrow and shame.
Swift may our bright beams go,
   In Jesus' name.
CHO.—We are little sunbeams, &c.

3. We are little sunbeams,
   With work to do,
We are little sunbeams,
   May we be true.
Where Jesus led the way,
   With footsteps sure,
There we may safely stay,
   There are secure.
CHO.—We are little Sunbeams, &c.
                    Dr. C. R. Blackall.

God is Love.

ORIOLA 117, Key of E flat; G. Tidings 58, H.
   Voices 42, S. S. Hosanna 99.

1. Come, let us all unite and sing,
   God is love, God is love ;
While heav'n and earth their praises bring;
   God is love.
Let ev'ry soul from sin awake,
   Their harps now from the willows take,
And sing with me, for Jesus' sake,
   God is love, God is love.

2. Oh, tell to earth's remotest bound,
   God is love, God is love.
In Christ I have redemption found,
   God is love.
His blood has wash'd my sins away ;
His spirit turns my night to day ;
And now my soul with joy can say,
   God is love, God is love.

3. How happy is our portion here !
   God is love, God is love.
His promises our spirits cheer,
   God is love
He is our sun and shield by day,
By night he near our tents will stay,

He will be with us all the way.
   God is love, God is love.

4. What though my heart and flesh shall
      fail ?
   God is love, God is love.
Through Christ I shall o'er death prevail,
   God is love.
Through Jordan's swell I will not fear ;
My Jesus will be with me there,
My head above the waves to bear.
   God is love, God is love.

Mary to the Saviour's Tomb.

Tune.---Martyn, Key of F.

1. Mary to the Saviour's tomb
   Hasted at the early dawn ;
Spice she brought, snd sweet perfume,
   But the Lord she loved, had gone.
For a while she lingering stood,
   Fill'd with sorrow and surprise,
Trembling, while a crystal flood
   Issued from her weeping eyes.

2. But her sorrows quickly fled
   When she heard his welcome voice :
Christ had risen from the dead ;
   Now he bids her heart rejoice :
What a change his word can make,
   Turning darkness into day !
Ye who weep for Jesus' sake,
   He will wipe your tears away.

A Light in the Window.

G. CHAIN 88, Key of A flat ; also Pil. Songs, 46.

1. There's a light in the window for thee,
      brother,
   There's a light in the window for thee ;
A dear one has moved to the mansions
      above,
   There's a light in the window for thee.
CHORUS.—A mansion in heaven we see,
   And a light in the window for thee ;
   A mansion in heaven we see,
   And a light in the window for thee.

2. There's a crown, and a robe, and a
      palm, brother.
   When from toil and from care you are
      free,
The Saviour has gone to prepare you a
      home,
   With a light in the window for thee.
CHO.—A mansion in heaven we see, &c.

3. O, watch, and be faithful, and pray,
      brother,
   All your journey o'er life's troubled sea;
Though afflictions assail you, and storms
      beat severe,
   There's a light in the window for thee.
CHO.—A mansion in heaven we see, &c.

Duett.

Words and Music by WILL HILL.

1. Come chil-dren to our Sab-bath school, At home no long-er stay,
2. Our teachers here are kind to us, We learn to sing and pray;
3. We learn to love each oth-er here; But should we go as-tray;
4. O may we nev-er, nev-er sin, While here on earth we stay;

We're hap-py as the lit-tle birds, O come and learn the way.
We learn of Je-sus who has died Our sins to wash a-way.
The lit-tle lambs he call-eth back From wan-der-ing a-way.
Our Sav-ior then with smiles will meet us, In that hap-py day.

Refrain.

Come and learn the way; O, come and learn the way;

Come and learn the way; O, come and learn the way;

Our teach-ers will be glad to meet you, Come, learn the way.

Our teach-ers will be glad to meet you, Come, learn the way.

I Want to be Like Jesus.

S. S. BELL No. 1 -32, Key of E flat.

1. I want to be like Jesus,
So lowly and so meek ;
For no one mark'd an angry word
That ever heard him speak.
I want to be like Jesus,
So frequently in prayer ;
Alone upon the mountain-top
He met his Father there.

2. I want to be like Jesus ;
I never, never find
That he, though persecuted, was
To any one unkind.
I want to be like Jesus,
Engaged in doing good,
So that of me it may be said,
" She hath done what she could."

3. I want to be like Jesus,
So lowly and so meek ;
For no one mark'd an angry word
That ever heard him speak.
Alas ! I'm not like Jesus,
As any one may see ;
O gentle Saviour, send thy grace,
And make me like to thee.

Jesus Paid it All.

G CENSER 12, Key of G ; also Glad Tidings 8, or
Musical Leaves 22, or Casket 9.

1. Nothing. either great or small,
Remains for me to do ;
Jesus died, and paid it all,—
Yes, all the debt I owe.
CHORUS.—Jesus paid it all,
All the debt I owe,
Jesus died, and paid it all,
Yes, all the debt I owe.

2. When he from his lofty throne
Stoop'd down to do and die,
Every thing was fully done,
" 'Tis finish'd !" was his cry.
CHO.—Jesus paid it all, &c.

3. Weary, working, plodding one,
Oh, wherefore toil you so ?
Cease your doing,—all was done,
Yes, ages long ago.
CHO.—Jesus paid it all, &c.

4. Till to Jesus' work you cling
Alone by simple faith,
" Doing " is a deadly thing,
Your " doing " ends in death.
CHO.—Jesus paid it all, &c.

5. Cast your deadly " doing " down,
Down, all at Jesus' feet ;
Stand in Him, in Him alone,
All glorious and complete.
CHO.—Jesus paid it all, &c.

Dare to do Right, &c.

G. CENSER 8, Key of E ; also Casket 14, Diadem
20.

1. Dare to do right, dare to be true,
You have a work that no other can do ;
Do it so bravely, so kindly, so well,
Angels will hasten the story to tell.
CHO.—Dare, dare, dare to do right !
Dare, dare, dare to be true !
Dare to be true, dare to be true !

2. Dare to do right, dare to be true,
Other men's failures can never save you :
Stand by your conscience, your honor,
your faith ;
Stand like a hero, and battle till death.
CHO.—Dare to do right, &c.

3. Dare to do right, dare to be true,
God, who created you, cares for you too,
Treasures the tears that his striving ones
shed,
Counts and protects every hair of your
head.
CHO.—Dare to do right, &c.

4. Dare to do right, dare to be true ;
Keep the great judgment-seat always in
view ;
Look at your work as you'll look at it then,
Scann'd by Jehovah, and angels, and men.
CHO.—Dare to do right, &c.

5. Dare to do right, dare to be true,
Jesus, your Saviour, will carry you through;
City, and mansion, and throne all in sight,
Can you not dare to be true and do right ?
CHO.—Dare to do right, &c.
Rev. J. L. Taylor.

Little Sunbeams Parting Song.

CHAPEL GEMS 80, Key of A flat.

1. Little sunbeams we'll away
From our Sabbath School to-day,
Hearts with love are bounding free,
Happier than birds are we.
CHO.—Teachers dear, a sweet good-bye,
As we leave you for our homes ;
Teachers dear, a sweet good-bye,
Till another Sabbath comes.

2. When the bells again shall call,
May our little sunbeams all,
Here in joy together meet,
Teachers, scholars, all to greet.
CHO.—Teachers dear, &c.

3. When our days on earth are o'er
And we reach the golden shore,
May each little sunbeam shine,
Brighter still, in light divine.
CHO.—Teachers, dear, &c.
Dr. C. R. Blackall.

Follow Me.

Words by MARY B. SLEIGHT.   H. R. PALMER.

1. Hark! the voice of Je - sus call - ing, "Fol - low me, fol - low me,"
2. Who will heed the ho - ly man-date, "Fol - low me, fol - low me,"
3. Hark - en lest he plead no long - er, "Fol - low me, fol - low me,"

Soft - ly thro' the si - lence fall - ing, "Fol - low, fol - low me,"
Leav - ing all things at his bid - ding, "Fol - low, fol - low me,"
Once a - gain, Oh hear him call - ing, "Fol - low, fol - low me,"

As of old He called the fish - ers, When He walked by Gal - li - lee,
Hark, that ten - der voice en - treat - ing, Mar - i - ners on life's rough sea.
Turn - ing swift at thy sweet summons, Ev - er - more dear Christ, would we

Still his pa - tient voice is plead - ing, "Fol - low, fol - low me."
Gent - ly, love - ing - ly, re - peat - ing, "Fol - low, fol - low me."
For thy love all else for - sak - ing, "Fol - low, fol - low Thee."

My Heavenly Home is Bright, &c.

G. CENSER 18, Key of F; also Oriola 28, Casket
106, H. Voices 227.

1. My heav'nly home is bright and fair,
   We'll be gather'd home,
No pain nor death can enter there,
   We'll be gather'd home.
   CHORUS—We'll wait till Jesus comes,
        We'll wait till Jesus comes,
        We'll wait till Jesus comes,
        And we'll be gather'd home.

2. Its glittering towers the sun outshine,
   We'll be gather'd home,
That heavenly mansion shall be mine,
   We'll be gather'd home.
   CHO.—We'll wait till Jesus comes, &c.

3. Let others seek a home below,
   We'll be gather'd home,
Which flames devour, or waves o'erflow,
   We'll be gather'd home.
   CHO.—We'll wait till Jesus comes, &c.

4. Be mine the happier lot to own,
   We'll be gather'd home,
A heavenly mansion near the throne,
   We'll be gather'd home.
   CHO.—We'll wait till Jesus comes, &c.

5. Then fail this earth, let stars decline,
   We'll be gather'd home,
And sun and moon refuse to shine,
   We'll be gather'd home.
   CHO.—We'll wait till Jesus comes, &c.

6. All nature sink and cease to be,
   We'll be gather'd home,
That heavenly mansion stands for me,
   We'll be gather'd home.
   CHO.—We'll wait till Jesus comes, &c.

Would You be as Angels Are.

S. S. BELL No. 1—16, Key of G.

1. Would you be as angels are,
   Sing, sing, sing his praise ;
Would you banish every care,
   Sing, sing, sing his praise ;
Like the lark upon the wing,
Like the warbling bird of spring,
Like the crystal spheres that ring,
   Sing, sing, sing his praise.

2. If the world upon you frown,
   Sing, sing, sing his praise ;
If you're left to sing alone,
   Sing, sing, sing his praise ;
If sad trials come to you,
As to every one they do,
For that they are blessings too,
   Sing, sing, sing his praise.

3. For his wondrous, dying love,
   Sing, sing, sing his praise ;
That he intercedes above,
   Sing, sing, sing his praise
Thus whene'er you come to die,

You shall soar beyond the sky,
And, with angel choirs on high,
   Sing, sing, sing his praise.

How Sweet is the Sabbath to Me.

S. S. HOSANNA 108, Key of G ; also Oriola 90, H.
Voices 206.

1. How sweet is the Sabbath to me,
   The day when the Saviour arose !
'Tis heaven his beauties to see,
   And in his soft arms to repose.
He knows I am weak and defiled,
   My life is but empty and vain ;
But if he will make me his child,
   I'll never forsake him again.

2. This day he invites me to come :
   How kindly he bids me draw near !
He offers me heaven for home,
   And wipes off the penitent tear :
He offers to pardon my sin,
   And keep me from every snare,
To sprinkle and cleanse me within,
   And show me his tenderest care.

3. I cannot, I must not refuse ;
   His goodness has conquer'd my heart ;
The Lord for my portion I choose,
   And bid all my folly depart.
How sweet is the Sabbath to me,
   The day my Redeemer arose !
'Tis heaven his beauties to see,
   And in his soft arms to repose.

Don't You Hear the Angels, &c.

S. S. BELL No. 2—6, Key of G.

1. Holy angels in their flight,
   Traverse over earth and sky,
Acts of kindness their delight,
   Winged with mercy as they fly.
CHO.—Don't you hear them ? coming over
   hill and plain,
Scattering music in their heavenly train !
Oh ! don't you hear the angels coming,
   singing as they come ?
Oh ! bear me angels, angels bear me home.

2. Tho' their forms we cannot see,
   They attend and guard our way,
Till we join their company
   In the fields of heavenly day.
   CHO.—Don't you hear, &c.

3. Had we but an angel's wing,
   And an angel's heart of flame,
Oh ! how sweetly would we ring
   Thro' the world the Saviour's name
   CHO.—Don't you hear, &c.

4. Yet methinks if I should die,
   And become an angel too,
I, perhaps, like them might fly,
   And the Saviour's bidding do.
   CHO.—Don't you hear, &c.

Words by Rob. Morris, L. L. D.

"*I saw the holy city.*" Rev. xxi—2.

1. Where flowers im - mor - tal bloom, We lit - tle pil - grims come,
2. Be - hold the star - ry walls— The bright and tower-ing halls!
3. Ah! blest and sure re - ward Its treas - u - ries af - ford!
4. Not long we'll tar - ry here;— But with good heart and cheer,

To view our prom - ised home, In sight of Heaven.
And hark! the an - gel calls— In sight of Heaven.
They speak a boun - teous Lord, In sight of Heaven.
Right on - ward we will bear— And go to Heaven.

Refrain.

Beau - ti - ful the vis - ion, Home of those now ris - en. Bright home of happiness,

Beau - ti - ful the vis - ion, Home of those now ris - en. Bright home of happiness,

Man - sion of bless - ed - ness, Cit - y of ho - li - ness, Where Je - sus lives.

Man - sion of bless - ed - ness, Cit - y of ho - li - ness, Where Je - sus lives.

Dear Sabbath School.

G. Chain 94, Key of E flat; also Diadem 12, or Oriola 64.

1. Yes, dear Sabbath School, I love thee :
Here I meet with friends most dear ;
None to scorn or feel above me,
None to dread with slavish fear ;
And the teachers,
And the teachers,
Kindly all my lessons hear ;
And the teachers,
And the teachers,
Kindly all my lessons hear.

2. Here I learn of richer treasures
Than the mines of earth afford ;
Earthly friends and earthly pleasures
Shall not keep me from the Lord :
Precious lessons
Here are spoken from his word.

3. Yet my heart is filled with wonder :
Parents, teachers, can you tell
Why neglected many wander,
When so near the school they dwell ?
Oh, invite them :
They will love the school so well.

4. I will go and tell those children
There is room for them and me ;
And to school will straightway bring them,
If persuaded, they will be :
I am thankful
That my friends invited me.

Home.

Tune.—" Sweet Home," Key of E flat ; also S. S. Hosanna 26.

1. Mid scenes of confusion and creature complaints,
How sweet to my soul is communion with saints,—
To find at the banquet of Mercy there's room,
And feel in the presence of Jesus at home !
Chorus.—Home, home ! sweet, sweet home !
Prepare me, dear Saviour, for glory, my home.

2. Sweet bonds, that unite all the children of peace,
And thrice-precious Jesus, whose love cannot cease !
Though oft from thy presence in sadness I roam,
I long to behold thee in glory at home.
Cho.—Home, home, &c.

3. I sigh from this body of sin to be free,
Which hinders my joy and communion with thee ;

Though now my temptation like billows may foam,
All, all will be peace when I'm with thee at home.
Cho.—Home, home, &c.

4. While here in the valley of conflict I stay,
Oh, give me submission and strength as my day ;
In all my afflictions to thee would I come,
Rejoicing in hope of my glorious home.
Cho.—Home, home, &c.

5. Whate'er thou deniest, oh, give me thy grace,
The Spirit's sure witness, and smiles of thy face ;
Endue me with patience to wait at thy throne
And find, even now, a sweet foretaste of home.
Cho.—Home, home, &c.

" Even Me."

G. Shower 83, Key of A flat ; also P. Songs 75, or Glad Tidings 84.

1. Lord, I hear of show'rs of blessings
Thou art scattering full and free,
Show'rs the thirsty land refreshing,
Let some droppings fall on me,—
Even me, even me,
Let some droppings fall on me.

2. Pass me not, O God, my Father,
Sinful though my heart may be ;
Thou might'st leave me, but the rather
Let thy mercy light on me,—
Even me, &c.

3. Pass me not, O gracious Saviour,
Let me live and cling to thee
Fain I'm longing for thy favor ;
Whilst thou'rt calling, call for me,—
Even me, &c.

4. Pass me not, O mighty Spirit,
Thou canst make the blind to see :
Witnesses of Jesus' merit,
Speak the word of power to me,—
Even me, &c.

5. Love of God, so pure and changeless ;
Blood of Christ, so rich and free ;
Grace of God, so rich and boundless,
Magnify it all in me,—
Even me, &c.

6. Pass me not, thy lost one bringing ;
Bind my heart, O Lord, to thee ;
Whilst the streams of life are springing,
Blessing others, oh, bless me,—
Even me, &c.

Words by Dr. C. R. Blackall. H. R. Palmer.

1. Glowing bright. and pleasant is the ho - ly day, When from world-ly du - ties,
2. Happy bells are ring-ing, calling us a - way, With their mer - ry chiming,
3. Joyous hearts are greeting, each to each to - day, While our dear Re - deem - er

glad we turn a - way, Blest be - yond all oth - ers with their work or play,
seem - ing e'er to say, "Come and join the sing - ing, haste without delay,
will - ing we o - bey, And with voi - ces mingling, here we praise and pray,

Refrain.

Is the ho - ly Sab - bath day.
'Tis the ho - ly Sab - bath day.
On this ho - ly Sab - bath day. Ev - er precious morn - ing,

when the Sav - ior rose, With his love a - dorn - ing, mak - ing friends of foes;

'Till the angels warning tells us time must close, Shall we love the Sabbath day.

Pleasant is the Sabbath Bell.

S. S BELL, No. 1—60, Key of G; also G. Chain 43, Oriola, 219, S. S. Hosanna, 24.

1. Pleasant is the Sabbath bell,
   In the light, in the light,
Seeming much of joy to tell,
   In the light of God.
But a music sweeter far,
   In the light, in the light,
Breathes where angel spirits are,
   In the light of God.
CHORUS.—Let us walk in the light,
   Walk in the light.
   Let us walk in the light,
   In the light of God.

2. Shall we ever rise to dwell,
   In the light, in the light,
Where immortal praises swell,
   In the light of God?
And can children ever go,
   In the light, in the light,
Where eternal Sabbaths glow,
   In the light of God?
   CHO.—Let us walk, &c.

3. Yes, that bliss our own may be,
   In the light, in the light,
All the good shall Jesus see,
   In the light of God.
For the good a rest remains,
   In the light, in the light,
Where the glorious Saviour reigns,
   In the light of God.
   CHO.—Let us walk, &c.

I Want to be an Angel.

S. S. BELL No. 1–32, Key of E flat; also Oriola 140, S. S. Hosanna 120.

1. I want to be an angel,
   And with the angels stand,
A crown upon my forehead,
   A harp within my hand :
There, right before my Saviour,
   So glorious and so bright,
I'd wake the sweetest music,
   And praise him day and night.

2. I never would be weary,
   Nor ever shed a tear,
Nor ever know a sorrow,
   Nor ever feel a fear ;
But, blessed, pure, and holy,
   I'd dwell in Jesus' sight,
And with ten thousand thousands
   Praise him both day and night.

3. I know I'm weak and sinful,
   But Jesus will forgive ;
For many little children
   Have gone to heaven to live.
Dear Saviour, when I languish,
   And lay me down to die,

Oh, send a shining angel
   To bear me to the sky.

4. Oh, there I'll be an angel,
   And with the angels stand,
A crown upon my forehead,
   A harp within my hand ;
And there, before my Saviour,
   So glorious and so bright,
I'll join the heavenly music,
   And praise him day and night.

I Now Believe.

G. CENSER 97, Key of G; also H. Voices 96, or G. Tidings 86.

1. There is a fountain, fill'd with blood
   Drawn from Immanuel's veins ;
And sinners, plunged beneath that flood,
   Lose all their guilty stains.
CHORUS.—I now believe, I do believe
   That Jesus died for me ;
   That on the cross he shed his blood,
   From sin to set me free.

2. The dying thief rejoiced to see
   That fountain in his day,
And there may I, though vile as he,
   Wash all my sins away.
CHO.—I now believe, I do believe, &c.

3. Thou dying Lamb, thy precious blood
   Shall never lose its power,
Till all the ransom'd Church of God
   Are saved, to sin no more.
CHO.—I now believe, I do believe, &c.

4. E'er since, by faith, I saw the stream
   Thy flowing wounds supply,
Redeeming love has been my theme,
   And shall be, till I die.
CHO.—I now believe, I do believe, &c.

5. Then, in a nobler, sweeter song,
   I'll sing thy power to save,
When this poor, lisping, stammering tongue
   Lies silent in the grave.
CHO.—I now believe, I do believe, &c.

Cross and Crown.

G. CHAIN 85, Key of B flat ; also H. Voices 80 New G. Chain 85.

1. Must Jesus bear the cross alone,
   And all the world go free ?
No : there's a cross for every one,
   And there's a cross for me.

2. How happy are the saints above,
   Who once went sorrowing here !
But now they taste unmingled love,
   And joy without a tear.

3. The consecrated cross I'll bear,
   Till death shall set me free,
And then go home, my crown to wear,—
   For there's a crown for me.

Father Rock Us.

Words by Miss M. B. Sleight.   Music by J. A. Butterfield.

A little girl saying her evening prayer, added the petition, "Lord, rock us in thy cradle."

1. Fath - er, rock us in thy cra - dle, We, thy lit - tle chil - dren, pray;
2. Fath - er, rock us in thy cra - dle; And a - bove each pil - low'd head,
3. Kiss us e'er we sleep, our Fath-er, With thy kiss of par - don blest;
4. Fath - er, rock us in thy cra - dle, When our day of life is done;
5. Then, O Fath - er, soft - ly rock us, In the cra - dle of thy love,

In the hush of eve we seek Thee, Wea - ry, with the long, long day.
Like a cur - tain soft and shadowy, Let thy watch - ful wing be spread.
And thro' all the still night watches, Give us each thy prom - is'd rest.
When the gath'ring shades have darkly Shut a - way the gol - den sun.
'Till our wond'ring eyes shall wak-en On thy per - fect day a - bove.

Refrain.

Fath - er, rock us in thy cra - dle, In the cra - dle of thy love;

Fath - er, rock us in thy cra - dle, In the cra - dle of thy love;

Ev - er with thy arms around us, Guide us to our home a - bove.

Ev - er with thy arms around us, Guide us to our home a - bove.

This Life is a Battle, &c.

H. Voices 179, Key of C ; also G. Chain 82.

1. This life is a battle 'gainst Satan and
     sin,
And we are the soldiers the vict'ry to win,
And Christ is the Captain of our little
     band ;
Whatever opposes, for him we will stand.
CHORUS.—Then stand up for Jesus, what-
     ever befall ;
On Calvary's mountain he stood for us all ;
Then stand up for Jesus, stand up for
     Jesus,
Stand up for Jesus, for Jesus.

2. To God for our armor we'll fail not to
     go,
He'll clothe us with truth and with righ-
     teousness too ;
The " gospel of peace " shall our footsteps
     attend,
And the " good shield of faith " from all
     harm shall defend.
CHO.—Then stand up for Jesus, &c.

3. Salvation our helmet, the Bible our
     sword,
Though wily our foes, we are " strong in
     the Lord ;"
While watching and praying our armor
     keeps bright,
Our Jesus will help us to stand for the
     right.
CHO.—Then stand up for Jesus, &c.

4. Though little temptations—the worst
     ones of all—
Will often beset us to make us to fall,
We'll stand up for Jesus ; and, when life
     is o'er,
For us he'll be standing on Jordan's bright
     shore.
CHO.—Then stand up for Jesus, &c.

Kind Words Can Never Die.

S. S. BELL No. 1—24, Key of E flat ; also S. S.
     Hosanna 86.

1. Kind words can never die :
     Heaven gave them birth ;
Wing'd with a smile, they fly
     All o'er the earth.
Kind words the angels brought,
Kind words our Saviour taught :—
Sweet melodies of thought !
     Who knows their worth ?
Kind words can never die, &c.

2. Kind deeds can never die :
     Though weak and small,
From his bright throne on high
     God sees them all ;
He doth reward with love
All those who faithful prove ;

Round them, where'er they move,
     Rich blessings fall.
Kind deeds can never die, &c.

3. God's word can never die ;
     Though fallen man
Oft dares its truth deny,—
     Dares it in vain.
God's word alone is pure
His promises are sure ;
Trust him, and rest secure
     Heaven you shall gain.
God's word can never die, &c.

4. Our souls can never die :
     God's word we trust ;
He to our bodies said,
     " Dust unto dust."
Saviour, our souls prepare
Thy happy home to share ;
Us to thy mansions bear
     When life is past.
Our souls can never die, &c.

When Shall we Meet Again.

UNITY IN S. S. HOSANNA 80, Key of E flat ; also
     H. Voices 147.

1. When shall we meet again,
     Meet ne'er to sever ?
When will peace wreathe her chain
     Round us forever ?
Our hearts will ne'er repose
Safe from each blast that blows
In this dark vale of woes,
     Never,—no, never.

2. When shall love freely flow,
     Pure as life's river ?
When shall sweet friendship glow
     Changeless forever,
Where joys celestial thrill,
Where bliss each heart shall fill,
And fears of parting chill
     Never,—no, never ?

3. Up to that world of light
     Take us, dear Saviour !
May we all there unite,
     Happy forever !
Where kindred spirits dwell,
There may our music swell,
And time our joys dispel
     Never,—no, never.

4. Soon shall we meet again,
     Meet ne'er to sever ;
Soon will peace wreathe her chain
     Round us forever ;
Our hearts will then repose,
Secure from worldly woes ;
Our songs of praise shall close
     Never,—no, never.

Words by Rev. H. C. M'Cook.

Music by Jas. M. North, by permission

1. I'm a pilgrim, pil-grim on the road, Lit-tle pil-grim on the road, To the
2. I was burden'd, burden'd with a load, Heav-y bur-den'd with a load, When I
3. I was wea-ry, wea-ry of the load, Ver-y wea-ry of the load, As I

cit-y of our God; I have left the way of sin That I had long wander'd
started on the road: 'Twas the sin that I had done; My own hand had laid it
totter'd o'er the road; But the Sa-vior took the pack From the lit-tle pil-grim's

Refrain.

in, And I'm presssing tow'rd the land, the land of glo-ry. On, on, on! I'm trav'ling
on, Ere I start-ed for the land, the land of glo-ry. On, on, &c.
back; And I'm traveling on with lightsome hearts to glory. On, on, &c.

on! On to glo-ry! on to glo-ry! I have left the way of sin, That I

long have wan-der'd in, And I'm trav'l-ing to the land the land of glo-ry.

4. There perils perils by the road.
Many perils, by the road;
But I trust the pilgrim's God;
With my staff believing pray'r,
Ev'ry danger I may dare,
While I travel to the land, the land of glory.
Chorus. On, on, on, &c.

5. Blessed Savior, Builder of the road,
Thou the way to me hast showed,
Grace to enter it bestowed;
O, support me day by day,
Giving strength for all the way,
That I journey tow'rd the land the land of glory.
On, on, on, &c.

Climbing up Zion's Hill.

SINGING PILGRIM 24, Key of F; also G. Censer 44, G. Tidings 122, Musical Leaves 24.

1. " I'm trying to climb up Zion's Hill,"
   For the Saviour whispers, " Love me ;"
Tho' all beneath is dark as death,
   Yet the stars are bright above me.
   Then upward still to Zion's hill,
To the land of joy and beauty,
   My path before, shines more and more,
As it nears the golden city.
CHORUS.—I'm climbing up Zion's hill,
     I'm climbing up Zion's hill,
Climbing, climbing, climbing up Zion's
   hill.

2. I know I'm but a little child,
   My strength will not protect me ;
But then I am the Saviour's lamb,
   And he will not neglect me.
   Then all the time I'll try to climb
This holy hill of Zion ;
   For I am sure the way is pure,
And on it comes " no lion."
     CHO.—I'm climbing up, &c.

3. Then come with me, we'll upward go,
   And climb this hill together ;
And as we walk, we'll sweetly talk,
   And sing as we go thither.
   Then mount up still God's holy hill,
Till we reach the pearly portals,
   Where raptured tongues proclaim the
     songs
Of the shining-robed immortals.
     CHO.—I'm climbing up, &c.

Beautiful River.

HAPPY VOICES 220, Key of E flat.

1. Shall we gather at the river
   Where bright angel feet have trod,
With its crystal tide forever
   Flowing by the throne of God ?
CHORUS.—Yes, we'll gather at the river,
   The beautiful, the beautiful river.
Gather with the saints at the river
   That flows by the throne of God.

2. On the margin of the river,
   Washing up its silver spray,
We will walk and worship ever,
   All the happy, golden day.
     CHO.—Yes, we'll gather, &c.

3. Ere we reach the shining river,
   Lay we every burden down ;
Grace our spirits will deliver,
   And provide a robe and crown.
     CHO.—Yes, we'll gather, &c.

4. At the smiling of the river,
   Mirror of the Saviour's face,
Saints whom death will never sever,
   Lift their songs of saving grace.
     CHO.—Yes, we'll gather, &c.

5. Soon we'll reach the silver river,
   Soon our pilgrimage will cease ;
Soon our happy hearts will quiver
   With the melody of peace.
     CHO.—Yes, we'll gather, &c.

One There is Above All Others.

SONG QUEEN 19, Key of D; also S. S. Hosanna 122, or H. Voices 66.

1. One there is above all others
   Well deserves the name of Friend ;
His is love beyond a brother's,
   Costly, free, and knows no end.

2. Which of all our friends, to save us
   Could or would have shed his blood ?
But this Saviour died to have us
   Reconciled, in him, to God.

3. When he lived on earth abased,
   Friend of sinners was his name ;
Now, above all glory raised,
   He rejoices in the same.

4. Oh for grace our hearts to soften !
   Teach us, Lord, at length to love ;
We, alas ! forget too often
   What a Friend we have above.

The Happy Land.

S. S. BELL No. 1—31, Key of E flat ; also S. S. Hosanna 63, Happy Voices 1.

1. There is a happy land,
   Far, far away ;
Where saints in glory stand,
   Bright, bright as day ;
Oh, how they sweetly sing,
Worthy is the Saviour King,
Loud let his praises ring,
   Praise, praise for aye !

2. Come to that happy land,
   Come, come away ;
Why will ye doubting stand,
   Why still delay ?
Oh, we shall happy be
When, from sin and sorrow free,
Lord, we shall live with thee,
   Clest, blest for aye.

3. Bright in that happy land
   Beams every eye ;
Kept by a Father's hand,
   Love cannot die.
Oh, then, to glory run,
Be a crown and kingdom won,
And bright above the sun
   We reign for aye.

The Old, Old Story.

W. H. DOANE.

1. Tell me the old, old sto - ry, Of un - seen things a - bove,
2. Tell me the sto - ry slow - ly, That I may take it in -
3. Tell me the sto - ry soft - ly, With ear - nest tones, and grave ;

4. Tell me the same old sto - ry, When you have cause to fear

Of Je - sus and his glo - ry, Of Je - sus and his love.
For I am weak and wea - ry, And help - less and de - filed.
Re - mem - ber! I'm the sin - ner Whom Je - sus came to save.

That this world's emp - ty glo - ry Is cost - ing me too dear.

Tell me the sto - ry sim - ply, As to a lit - tle child,
Tell me the sto - ry oft - en, For I for - get so soon!
Tell me that sto - ry al - ways, If you would real - ly be,

Yes, and when that world's glo - ry Is dawn - ing on my soul,

That won - der - ful re - demp - tion God's rem - e - dy for sin.
The "ear - ly dew" of morn - ing Has passed a - way at noon
In a - ny time of trou - ble, A com - fort - er to me.

Tell me the old, old sto - ry, "Christ Je - sus makes thee whole."

Refrain.

Tell me the old, old sto - ry, Tell me the old, old sto - ry.

Tell me the old, old sto - ry, Of Je - sus and his love.

Do Good.

G. CENSER 38, Key of D.

1. Do good ! do good ! there's ever a way,
A way where there's ever a will,
Don't wait till to-morrow, but do it to-
day,
And to-day, when the morrow comes,
still.
(Repeat first Stanza as Chorus.)

2. God careth for all, and his glorious sun
Shines alike on the rich and the poor ;
Be thou like Him, and bless every one,
And thou'lt be rewarded sure.
CHO.—Do good, &c.

3. Do good ! do good ! we are never too
young
To be useful in many a way ;
For all have a heart, and a hand, and a
tongue,
To feel, and to labor, and pray.
CHO.—Do good, &c.

4. If we have but a moment, that mo-
ment employ,
To pluck the young brands from the
flame ;
We may change their deep guilt to a
Christian's full joy,
And save them for ever from shame.
CHO.—Do good, &c.

5. What joy, what joy will the least of us
know,
When called to our father's abode,
To find that beside us in glory there stands
Those whom we first placed on the road!
CHO.—Do good, &c.

6. Then seek in the highways and byways
of earth,
And bring in the lowly to feast :
Remember, in heaven the greatest may be
The one who on earth was the least.
CHO.—Do good, &c.

Sweet Story.

ORIOLA 133, Key of D.

1. I think when I read that sweet story of
old,
When Jesus was here among men,
How he call'd little children as lambs to
his fold,
I should like to have been with them
then.

2. I wish that his hands had been placed
on my head,
That his arm had been thrown around
me,
And that I might have seen his kind look
when he said,
" Let the little ones come unto me."

3. Yet still to his footstool in prayer I may
go,
And ask for a share in his love ;
And if I thus earnestly seek him below,
I shall see him and hear him above.

4. In that beautiful place he has gone to
prepare
For all who are wash'd and forgiven :
And many dear children are gathering
there,
" For of such is the kingdom of heaven."

The Child's Desire.

Tune.—" I Want to be an Angel." S. S. Bell No·
1—32, Key of D.

1. I want to BE like Jesus,
All gentle, pure, and mild,
His seal upon my forehead,
And owned as His dear child ;
My heart, so weak and sinful,
All changed by grace divine,
And all my life to serve Him,
And ever call Him mine !

2. I want to DO like Jesus,—
To mark each passing day
With deeds of love and mercy,
Or cheer some lonely way,
Speak gentle words of counsel,
Avoid e'en secret sin,
And to my precious Saviour,
The lost ones seek to win.

3. I want to LIVE like Jesus,
Whose words with love were fraught ;
I want to find His favor,
By Him be truly taught :
Oh ! then I'm sure that ever,
His hand will guide me on,
Until the Heavenly portals,
And Glory, shall be won !

4. There I shall REIGN with Jesus,
And see Him face to face,—
There, in His love forever,
Shall triumph through His grace ;
My robe so pure and spotless,
My harp and crown so bright,
I shall through endless ages,
His praises sing aright !

5. Oh ! MAKE me, then, like Jesus,
My Father, God, above,
And change my heart so sinful—
Oh ! change it by Thy love !
Then I shall live like Jesus,
Be gentle, pure, and mild,
And with Him reign forever,
And be for aye his child !
Dr. C. R. Blackall.

Geo. F. Root.

1. Who will meet me when I die? Who will lead me
2. When my Sa - vior from on high, Calls my spir - it

8. Who will hush my trem - bling heart? Who will heaven - ly

to the sky? Who will love me in that land? In that spir - it
to the sky? Who will meet me on the strand, Of that spir - it

joy im - part? Who will love me in that land? In that spir - it

Refrain.

land. An - gels bright will meet me, An - gels bright, An - gels bright;
land? An - gels bright, &c.

land? An - gels bright, will meet me, An - gels bright; An - gels bright;

An - gels bright will meet me, In that spir - it land.

An - gels bright will meet me, In that spir - it land.

*From "Chapel Gems," by permission of Root & Cady.

Here we Throng, &c.

S. S. BELL No. 1—22, Key of E flat.

1. Here we throng to praise the Lord ;
Listen now, listen now,
Here we throng to praise the Lord,
With our infant lays.
He who once lay in a manger,
Now enthroned, our blest Redeemer,
With a father's love has said,
He'd accept our praise.

2. "Let young children come to me,"
Jesus said, Jesus said ;
"Let young children come to me,
And forbid them not—
For of such," the Saviour told them,
"Is composed my heavenly kingdom."
What a rapturous thought it is,
Christ forgets us not !

3. Let us love, and now adore ;
Love him now, love him now,
Let us love, and now adore,
In our youthful strength.
Let us never grieve our Saviour,
Who hath died to win us favor—
Ah ! this thought should melt our hearts—
Children's hearts can melt.

4. But we'll have a joyous song,
Joyous song, joyous song ;
But we'll have a joyous song
For our jubilee.
Jesus lives and reigns for ever ;
This will make us joyous ever.
Saviour, hear this praise to thee,
Who remembered me.

The Sunday School Army.

S. S. BELL No. 1—29, Key of G.

1. O, do not be discouraged,
For Jesus is your friend ;
O, do not be discouraged,
For Jesus is your friend,
He will give you grace to conquer,
He will give you grace to conquer,
And keep you to the end.
CHORUS.—I am glad I'm in this army,
Yes, I'm glad I'm in this army,
Yes, I'm glad I'm in this army,
And I'll battle for the school.

2. Fight on, ye little soldiers,
The battle you shall win,
Fight on, ye little soldiers,
The battle you shall win ;
For the Saviour is your Captain,
For the Saviour is your Captain,
And he hath vanquished sin,
CHO.—I am glad I'm in, &c.

3. And when the conflict's over,
Before him you shall stand ;

And when the conflict's over,
Before him you shall stand ;
You shall sing his praise for ever,
You shall sing his praise for ever,
In Canaan's happy land.

I Have a Father, &c.

S. S. BELL No. 1—4, Key of E flat.

1. I have a Father in the promised land,
I have a Father in the promised land,
My Father calls me, I must go
To meet Him in the promised land,
CHORUS,—I'll away, I'll away to the prom-
ised land,
I'll away, I'll away to the promised land,
My Father calls me, I must go
To meet Him in the promised land.

2. I have a Saviour in the promised land,
I have a Saviour in the promised land,
My Saviour calls me, I must go
To meet Him in the promised land.
CHO.—I'll away, I'll away to the, &c.

3. I have a crown in the promised land,
I have a crown in the promised land,
When Jesus calls me, I must go
To wear it in the promised land.
CHO.—I'll away, I'll away to the, &c.

The Land of Canaan.

S. S. BELL No. 1—14, Key of F.

1. Together let us sweetly live,
I am bound for the land of Canaan ;
Together let us sweetly die,
I am bound for the land of Canaan.
CHORUS.—O Canaan, bright Canaan,
I am bound for the land of Canaan ;
O Canaan, is my happy home,
I am bound for the land of Canaan.

2. If you get there before I do,
I am bound for the land of Canaan ;
Then praise the Lord, I'm coming too,
I am bound for the land of Canaan.
CHO.—O Canaan, &c.

3. Part of my friends the prize have won,
I am bound for the land of Canaan ;
And I'm resolved to travel on,
I am bound for the land of Canaan.
CHO.—O Canaan, &c.

4. Then come with me, beloved friend,
I am bound for the land of Canaan ;
The joys of heaven shall never end,
I am bound for the land of Canaan.
CHO.—O Canaan, &c.

5. Our songs of praise shall fill the skies,
I am bound for the land of Canaan ;
While higher still our joys they rise,
I am bound for the land of Canaan.
CHO.—O Canaan, &c.

Beautiful Home.

Words by FRANK FOREST.

Music by H. R. PALMER.

1. There is a home e - ter - nal Beau-ti-ful and bright, Where sweet joys su-per-nal
2. Flow-ers for-ev-er are springing In that home so fair Thousands of children are singing
3. Soon shall I join that an-them Far beyond the sky Je - sus became my ran-som.

Never are dim'd by night; White-robed an-gels are singing Ever around the bright
Praises to Je - sus there How they swell the glad anthems Ever around the bright
Why should I fear to die ; Soon my eyes will behold him Seated up-on the bright

throne When O when shall I see thee Beau - ti - ful beau - ti - ful home.
throne When O when shall I see thee Beau - ti - ful beau - ti - ful home.
throne Then, O then shall I see thee Beau - ti - ful beau - ti - ful home.

Refrain.

Beau - ti - ful home   Beau - ti - ful home.

Home beau - ti - ful home.   Bright beau-ti - ful home.

Beau-ti - ful home   Beau - ti - ful home.

Repeat chorus pp.

Home, home of our Sav - ior Beau - ti - ful Beau - ti - ful home.

Home home of our Sav - ior Bright   beau-ti - ful home,

Beau - ti - ful beau - ti - ful home.

Charity.

S. S. BELL No. 1—111, Key of E flat.

Meek and lowly, pure and holy,
  Chief among the " blessed three :"
Turning sadness into gladness,
  Heav'n born art thou, Charity.
Pity reigneth in thy bosom,
  Kindness reigneth o'er thy heart,
Gentle thoughts alone can sway thee,
  Judgment hath in thee no part.

Hoping ever, failing never,
  Tho' deceived, believing still ;
Long abiding, all confiding,
  To thy heavenly Father's will.
Never weary of well-doing,
  Never fearful of the end,
Claiming all mankind as brothers,
  Thou dost all mankind befriend.

Little Drops of Water.

S. S. BELL No. 1—21, Key of C.

1. Little drops of water,
  Little grains of sand,
Make the mighty ocean,
  And the beauteous land.

2. And the little moments,
  Humble tho' they be,
Make the mighty ages
  Of eternity.

3. So our little errors
  Lead the soul away
From the paths of virtue
  Oft in sin to stray.

4. Little deeds of kindness,
  Little words of love,
Make our earth an Eden
  Like the heaven above.

5 Little seeds of mercy,
  Sown by youthful hands,
Grow to bless the nations,
  Far in heathen lands.

Saviour Like a Shepherd, &c.

SICILIAN HYMN, Key of D ; also G. Chain 94, G. Harp 100.

1. Saviour, like a shepherd lead us :
  Much we need thy tender care ;
In thy pleasant pastures feed us,
  For our use thy folds prepare.
    Blessed Jesus !
Thou hast bought us, thine we are.

2. We are thine : do thou befriend us,
  Be the guardian of our way ;
Keep thy flock, from sin defend us,
  Seek us when we go astray.
    Blessed Jesus !
Hear young children when they pray.

3. Thou hast promised to receive us,
  Poor and sinful though we be ;
Thou hast mercy to relieve us,
  Grace to cleanse, and power to free.
    Blessed Jesus !
Let us early turn to thee.

4. Early let us seek thy favor,
  Early let us do thy will ;
Holy Lord, our only Saviour,
  With thy grace our bosom fill.
    Blessed Jesus !
Thou hast loved us, love us still.

Infant Class Song.

Tune.—" Feed my Lambs," Chapel Gems 94, Key of B flat.

Jesus loved the little children,
  When he dwelt on earth below
In his arms he took them gently,
  And a blessing did bestow ;
He doth love *us*, too, his children,
  We may all his blessing share,
If we heed him and obey him,
  He will give us tenderest care.

    CHANT, Key of E flat.

" Come to me,"—his | voice is | calling,--||
  " Freely come, ye | need not | fear !"||
We have come, dear Saviour, pleading,
  Hear, oh, hear, the | infant's | prayer :

Jesus, be our | Shepherd, | guide us,||
  Keep us in thine | arms of | love||
Safe from all of sin defend us,
  Bring us to thy | home a | bove.
    Amen.

    Dr. C. R. Blackall.

Call to Praise.

S. S. BELL, No. 1—60, Key of G ; also G. Chain 43.

1. Children of the heavenly King,
  In the light, in the light,
As we journey, sweetly sing,
  In the light of God ;
Sing our Saviour's worthy praise,
  In the light, in the light,
Glorious in his works and ways,
  In the light of God.
    CHO.—Let us walk, &c.

2. We are traveling home to God,
  In the light, in the light,
In the way our fathers trod,
  In the light of God ;
They are happy now, and we,
  In the light, in the light,
Soon their happiness shall see,
  In the light of God.
    CHO.—Let us walk, &c.

Words by Rob. Morris. L. L. D.

Music by H. R. Palmer,

1. When e'er you see a school boy who climbs the orchard fence, Or sneaks around the corner to
2. When e'er you see him loaf - ing, who ought to be at school, Or playing the idle tru - ant a-
3. Whene'er you see him fighting or brawling in the street, Or playing the schoolboy bully, the
4. When e'er you hear him swearing, or saying the naughty word, Or telling a lie or tattling of
5. Don't let the devil lead him in ways of burning shame. Speak up, ye gallant Captain and
6. But when you see him doing the thing he ought to do, And when you hear him speaking the

Refrain.

steal the apple and quince,
gainst the teach-er's rule. Tell him to halt ! tell him to halt ! Whatever may be his fault.
mean-est thing you meet.

something he has heard.
call him by his name. Tell him to halt ! tell him to halt ! Whatever may be his fault ;
word so good and true.

For last stanza.   Tell him to march, tell him to march, Right under the Christian arch.

Tell him to halt ! tell him to halt ! Whatever may be his fault ; Play up the lit - tle

Tell him to halt ! tell him to halt ! Whatever may be his fault ; Play up the lit - tle

Tell him to march ! tell him to march ! Right under the Christian arch ; Play up the lit-tle

Captain, The brave and gallant Captain, And tell him to halt !   Halt ! halt ! halt.

Captain, The brave and gallant Captain, And tell him to halt !   Halt ! halt ! halt.

Captain, The brave and gallant Captain, And tell him to march !   March ! march ! march.

We are out on the Ocean,

OLIVE BRANCH 284, Key of E flat; also G. Chain 87, S. S. Hosanna 56, Oriola 98,

1. We are out on an ocean sailing ;
Homeward bound we smoothly glide ;
We are out on an ocean, sailing
To a home beyond the tide.
CHORUS.—All the storms will soon be over ;
Then we'll anchor in the harbor ;
We are out on an ocean, sailing
To a home beyond the tide.

2. Millions now are safely landed
Over on the golden shore ;
Millions more are on their journey,
Yet there's room for millions more.
CHO.—All the storms, &c.

3. Come on board, oh, ship for glory,
Be in haste, make up your mind,
For our vessel's weighing anchor,
And you may be left behind.
CHO.—All the storms, &c.

4. When we all are safely anchor'd,
We will shout our journey o'er,
We will walk about the city
And will sing for evermore.
CHO.—All the storms, &c.

Oh, Come, Let us Sing,

S. S. BELL No. 1—1. Key of D ; also Oriola 210.

1. Oh, come, let us sing,
Our youthful hearts now swelling,
To God above, a God of love,—
Oh, come, let us sing !
Our joyful spirits glad and free,
With high emotions rise to thee
In heavenly melody,—
Oh, come, let us sing !

2. The full notes prolong,
Our festal celebrating,
We hail the day with cheerful lay,
And full notes prolong,
Both cheerful youth and silvery age,
And childhood pure, the gay, the sage,
These thrilling scenes engage
Full notes to prolong.

3. Oh, swell, swell the song,
His praises oft repeating :
His Son he gave our souls to save,—
Oh, swell, swell the song.
The humble heart's devotion bring,
Whence gushing streams of love do spring,
And make the welkin ring
With sweet-swelling song.

4. We'll chant, chant his praise,
Our lofty strains now blending,
A tribute bring to Christ our king,
And chant, chant his praise !
Our Saviour Prince was crucified,

"'Tis finish'd !" then he meekly cried,
And bow'd his head and died,—
Then chant, chant his praise !

"Just Now,"

G. CENSER 70, Key of F ; also Casket 69.

1. Come to Jesus just now, &c.
"Come unto me, all ye that labor and are heavy laden and I will give you rest."—*Matt* 11 : 28.

2. He will save you just now, &c.
"Believe on the Lord Jesus Christ, and thou shalt be saved "—*Acts* 16 : 31.

3. Oh, believe him just now, &c.
"God so loved the world that he gave his only begotten Son, that whosoever believeth in him should not perish, but have everlasting life."—*John* 3 : 16.

4. He is able.
"He is able to save them to the uttermost that come unto God by him, seeing he ever liveth to make intercession for us."—*Heb.* 7 : 25.

5. He is willing.
"The Lord is long-suffering to usward, not willing that any should perish, but that all, should come to repentance."—*2 Pet.* 3 : 9.

6. He'll receive you.
"Him that cometh to me I will in no wise cast out."—*John* 6 : 37.

7. Then flee to Jesus.
"Flee from the wrath to come."—*Matt.* 3 : 7.

8. Call unto him.
"Whosoever shall call on the name of the Lord shall be saved."—*Acts* 2 : 21.

9. Mercy on me.
"Jesus, thou Son of David, have mercy on me."—*Mark* 10 : 47.

The Sunday School,

G. CHAIN 4, Key of G; also G. Tidings 123, Happy Voices 97, Oriola 144.

1. The Sunday School, that blessed place!
Oh, I would rather stay
Within its walls, a child of grace,
Than spend my hours in play.
The Sunday School, the Sunday School,
Oh, 'tis the place I love,
For there I learn the golden rule
Which leads to joys above.

2. 'Tis there I learn that Jesus died
For sinners such as I ;
Oh, what has all the world beside,
That I should prize so high ?
The Sunday School, &c.

3. Then let our grateful tribute rise,
And songs of praise be given,
To Him who dwells above the skies,
For such a blessing given.
The Sunday School, &c.

4. And welcome, then, the Sunday School!
We'll read, and sing, and pray,
That we may keep the golden rule,
And never from it stray.
The Sunday School, &c.

An aged christian, when asked what he was doing, replied, "Only waiting."

solo.

Arr. and adapted by H. R. PALMER.

1. On - ly wait-ing 'till the shadows Are a lit - tle long-er grown;
2. On - ly wait-ing 'till the reap-ers Have their last sheaf gath-er'd home;
3. On - ly wait-ing 'till the an - gels O - pen wide the mys-tic gate,
4. On - ly wait-ing 'till the shadows Are a lit - tle long-er grown;

Accompaniment soft.

On - ly wait-ing 'till the glimmer Of the day's last beam is flown,
For the Summer - time is end - ed, And the Au - tumn winds have come,
At whose feet I long have lingered, Wea - ry, poor, and des - o - late,
On - ly wait-ing 'till the glimmer Of the day's last beam is flown;

Duet.   *ad lib.*

'Till the night of earth is fad - ed, From the heart once full of day,
Quick-ly, reap-ers, gath - er quickly, The last ripe hours of my heart,
E - ven now I hear their footsteps, And their voices far a - way,
Then from out the gath'ring darkness, Ho - ly, deathless stars will rise,

Quartet.

'Till the stars of heav'n are break-ing, Thro' the twi - light soft and grey,
For the bloom of life is wither'd And I hast-en to de - part.

If they call me I am wait-ing, On - ly wait-ing to o - bey.
By whose light my soul will glad - ly Wing its pas - sage to the skies.

Where, O Where, are the, &c.

Oriola 236, Key of F.

1. Where, O where, are the Hebrew chil-
dren—
Where, O where, are the Hebrew children,
Who were cast in the furnace of fire ?
Safe now in the promised land.
CHO.—By and by we'll go home to meet
them,
By and by we'll go home to meet them,
By and by we'll go home to meet them,
'Way o'er in the promised land.

2. Where, O where, is the good Elijah,
Where, O where, is the good Elijah,
Who went up in a chariot of fire ?
Safe now in the promised land.
CHO.—By and by, &c.

3. Where, O where is the prophet Daniel--
Where, O where is the prophet Daniel,
Who was cast in the den of lions ?
Safe now in the promised land.
CHO.—By and by, &c.

4. Where, O where is the weeping Mary—
Where, O where is the weeping Mary,
Who was first at the tomb of Jesus ?
Safe now in the promised land.
CHO.—By and by, &c.'

5. Where, O where is the martyred
Stephen—
Where, O where is the martyred Stephen,
Who was stoned for his love to Jesus ?
Safe now in the promised land.
CHO.—By and by, &c.

6. Where, O where is the blessed Jesus,
Where, O where is the blessed Jesus,
Who was pierced on the mount of Cal-
vary ?
Safe now in the promised land.
CHO.—By and by, &c.

Marching Along.

G. CHAIN 112, Key of C; also S. S. Hosanna 162,
Shining Star 80.

1. The children are gath'ring from near
and from far,
The trumpet is sounding the call for the
war,
The conflict is raging, 'twill be fearful and
long,
We'll gird on our armor and be marching
along.
CHORUS.
Marching along, we are marching along,
Gird on the armor and be marching along,
The conflict is raging, 'twill be fearful and
long,
Then gird on the armor and be marching
along.

2. The foe is before us in battle array,
But let us not waver nor turn from the
way :
The Lord is our strength, be this ever our
song,
With courage and faith we are marching
along.
CHO.—Marching along, &c.

3. We've 'listed for life, and will camp on
the field,
With Christ as our Captain we never will
yield ;
The "sword of the Spirit," both trusty
and strong,
We'll hold in our hands as we're marching along.
CHO.—Marching along, &c.

4. Through conflicts and trials our crowns
we must win, •
For here we contend 'gainst temptation
and sin.
But one thing assures us, we cannot go
wrong,
If trusting our Saviour, while marching
along,
CHO.—Marching along, &c.
R. P. Clark.

Come Thou Fount, &c.

G. CENSER 101, Key of E.

1. Come, thou Fount of every blessing,
Tune my heart to sing thy grace ;
Streams of mercy, never ceasing,
Call for songs of loudest praise ;
CHORUS.—I love Jesus, hallelujah,
I love Jesus, yes, I do,
I do love Jesus ; he's my Saviour,
Jesus smiles and loves me too.

2. Teach me some melodious sonnet,
Sung by flaming tongues above ;
Praise the mount,—I'm fix'd upon it,—
Mount of God's unchanging love.
CHO.—I love Jesus, &c.

3. Jesus sought me when a stranger,
Wandering from the fold of God :
He, to rescue me from danger
Interposed his precious blood.
CHO.—I love Jesus, &c.

4. Oh, to grace how great a debtor
Daily I'm constrain'd to be !
Let that grace now, like a fetter,
Bind my wandering soul to thee :
CHO.—I love Jesus, &c.

5. Prone to wander, Lord, I feel it,—
Prone to leave the God I love ;
Here's my heart,—oh, take and seal it.
Seal it from thy courts above.
CHO.—I love Jesus, &c.

Angry Words.

Inscribed to the Sunday School of Plymouth Church.

By H. R. PALMER.

1. An - gry words! O let them nev - er From the tongue un - bri - dled slip:
2. Love is much too pure and ho - ly; Friend-ship is too sa - cred far,
3. An - gry words are light - ly spo - ken; Bit-terest thoughts are rash - ly stirred:

May the heart's best im - pulse ev - er Check them, e'er they soil the lip.
For a mo - ment's reck-less fol - ly Thus to des - o - late and mar.
Bright-est links of life are brok-en By a sin - gle an - gry word.

Chorus.

"Love each other," "Love each other," 'Tis thy Father's blest command,

"Love one an - oth - er," Thus saith the Sav-ior, Children obey thy Father's blest command,

"Love each other," "Love each other," 'Tis thy Father's blest command,

"Love each other," "Love each other," 'Tis His blest command.

"Love one an - oth - er" Thus saith the Sav-ior Chil-dren o-bey His blest com-mand.

"Love each other," "Love each other," 'Tis His blest command.

Say Brothers Will You Meet Us.

S. S. HOSANNA 13, Key of B flat.

1. Say, brothers, will you meet us,
Say, brothers, will you meet us,
Say, brothers, will you meet us,
On Canaan's happy shore ?
COHRUS.—Glory, glory, hallelujah,
　　　　Glory, glory, hallelujah,
　　　　Glory, glory, hallelujah,
　　　　For ever, evermore.

2. By the grace of God, we'll meet you,
By the grace of God, we'll meet you,
By the grace of God, we'll meet you,
On Canaan's happy shore.
CHO.—Glory, &c.

3. Jesus lives and reigns forever,
Jesus lives and reigns forever,
Jesus lives and reigns forever,
On Canaan's happy shore.
CHO.—Glory, &c.

4. Thus we'll tell the wondrous story,
Thus we'll tell the wondrous story,
Thus we'll tell the wondrous story,
On Canaan's happy shore.
CHO.—Glory, &c.

5. " Souls redeem'd and sins forgiven,"
" Souls redeem'd and sins forgiven,"
" Souls redeem'd and sins forgiven,"
On Canaan's happy shore.
CHO.—Glory, &c.

6. Glory in the highest glory,
Glory in the highest glory,
Glory in the highest glory,
On Canaan's happy shore.
CHO.—Glory, &c.

We are Coming, Blessed Saviour.

G. CENSER 17, Key of D ; also Casket 80, Musical
Leaves 33.

1. We are coming, blessed Saviour,
We hear thy gentle voice ;
We would be thine forever,
And in thy love rejoice.
CHORUS.—We are coming, we are coming,
　　　　We are coming, blessed Saviour,
　　　　We are coming, we are coming,
　　　　We hear thy gentle voice.

2. We are coming, blessed Saviour,
To meet that happy band,
And sing with them forever,
And in thy presence stand.
CHO.—We are coming, &c.
　　　　To meet that happy band.

3. We are coming, blessed Saviour,
Our Father's house we see,—
A glorious mansion ever
For children young as we.

CHO.—We are coming, &c.
　　　　Our Father's house we see.

4. We are coming, blessed Saviour,
That happy home is ours ;
If here we gain thy favor,
We'll reach those fragrant bowers.
CHO.—We are coming, &c.
　　　　That happy home is ours.

5. We are coming, blessed Saviour,
To crown our Jesus King,
And then with angels ever
His praises we will sing.
CHO.—We are coming, &c.
　　　　To crown our Jesus King.

Marching On.

HAPPY VOICES 139, Key of D ; also G. Censer 96

1. Marching on, marching on, glad as
　　birds on the wing,
Come the bright ranks of soldiers from
　　near and from far ;
Happy hearts full of song 'neath our ban-
　　ners we bring,
We are soldiers of Zion prepared for the
　　war.
CHORUS.—Marching on, marching on,
Sound the battle-cry, sound the battle-cry !
For the Saviour is before us, and for him
　　we draw the sword ;
Marching on, marching on,
Shout the victory, the victory, the victory !
We will end the battle singing hallelujah
　　to the Lamb.

2. Pressing on, pressing on, to the din of
　　the fray,
With the firm tread of faith to the bat-
　　tle we go ;
Mid the cheering of angels, our ranks
　　march away,
With our flags pointing ever right on
　　tow'rds the foe.
CHO.—Marching on, &c.

3. Fighting on, fighting on, in the midst
　　of the strife,
At the call of our Captain, we draw
　　ev'ry sword ;
We are battling for God, we are strug-
　　gling for life,
Let us strike every sinner that fights
　　'gainst the Lord.
CHO.—Marching on, &c.

4. Singing on, singing on, from the battle
　　we come,
Ev'ry flag bears a wreath, ev'ry soldier
　　renown ;
Heavenly angels are waiting to welcome
　　us home,
And the Saviour will give us a robe and
　　a crown.
CHO.—Marching on, &c.

L. B. Marsh.

1. The Sab-bath morn is break-ing, The Sab-bath bells are wak - ing,
2. 'Tis here we join in sing - ing, The songs of love re - deem - ing,
3. Our teach-ers we'll re-mem - ber; Ten thou-sand thanks we ren - der,

4. But ah! life's sun-ny morn-ing With all its sweet a - dorn - ing,
5. Then may we all re-mem - ber To strive our hearts to ren - der,

Our homes with joy for-sak - ing, To join the Sab-bath School.
Our lit - tle offer-ings bring-ing, Ho-san-nas to our King.
For thoughts of us so ten - der, While in our Sab-bath School.

Like ear - ly blos-soms fall - ing. Will soon have passed a - way.
While now so young and ten - der, To Christ, our heaven-ly King.

Refrain.

Shout and sing; Shout and sing; We hail the Sab-bath School!

Shout and sing; Shout and sing; We hail the Sab-bath School!

Shout and sing; Shout and sing; We hail the Sab-bath School!

Shout and sing; Shout and sing; We hail the Sab-bath School!

There is a Land, &c.

VARNA, IN S. S. HOSANNA 143, Key of E flat.

1. There is a land of pure delight,
   Where saints immortal reign;
Eternal day excludes the night,
   And pleasures banish pain.

2. There everlasting spring abides,
   And never-withering flowers;
Death, like a narrow sea divides
   This heavenly land from ours.

3. Sweet fields beyond the swelling flood
   Stand dress'd in living green;
So to the Jews old Canaan stood,
   While Jordan roll'd between.

4. Could we but climb where Moses stood
   And view the landscape o'er,
Not Jordan's stream, nor death's cold
   flood,
   Should fright us from the shore.

Yes, We Trust, &c.

ZION, IN S. S. HOSANNA 127, Key of D; or Fresh Laurels 11.

1. Yes! we trust the day is breaking,
   Joyful times are near at hand;
God—the mighty God—is speaking,
   By his word, in every land:
      When he chooses,
   Darkness flies at his command.

2. Oh, 'tis pleasant, 'tis reviving
   To our hearts, to hear, each day,
Joyful news from far arriving,   ·
   How the gospel wins its way,
      Those enlightening
   Who in death and darkness lay.

3. God of Jacob, high and glorious,
   Let thy people see thy hand;
Let the gospel be victorious
   Through the world, in every land;
      Then shall idols
   Perish, Lord, at thy command.

Something for Children to do.

Tune.—"There'll be something to do." G. Censer, 80, Key of B flat.

1. There is something on earth for the
      children to do—
For each Child that is striving to be
Like the One who once murmured in ac-
      cents of love
"Let the little ones come unto me."
CHORUS.—There is something to do, there
      is something to do;
There is something for children to do.
On this beautiful earth where the Saviour
      had birth,
There is something for children to do.

2. There are sweet winning words to the
      weary and sad
By their glad loving lips to be said;
There are hearts that are waiting by some
      little hand
Unto Jesus the Lord to be led.
   CHO.—There is something to do, &c.

3. There are lessons to learn both at home
      and at school;
There are battles to fight for the right;
There's a watch to be kept over temper
      and tongue
And God's help to be asked day and
      night.
   CHO.—There is something to do, &c.

4. There are smiles to be given, kind deeds
      to be done,
Gentle words to be dropped by the way—
For the Child that is seeking to follow the
      Lord
There is something to do every day.
   CHO.—There is something to do, &c.
                        Mary B. Sleight.

Child of Sin and Sorrow.

S. S. HOSANNA 103, Key of B flat; also Oriola 197 or Glad Tidings 57.

1. Child of sin and sorrow, fill'd with dis-
      may,
Wait not for to-morrow; yield thee to-day.
      Heaven bids thee come,
      While yet there's room.
      Child of sin and sorrow,
      Hear and obey.

2. Child of sin and sorrow, why wilt thou
      die?
Come, while thou canst borrow help
      from on high:
      Grieve not that love
      Which from above—
      Child of sin and sorrow—
      Would bring thee nigh.

3. Child of sin and sorrow, where wilt
      thou flee
Through that long to-morrow, eternity?
      Exiled from home,
      Darkly to roam,—
      Child of sin and sorrow,
      Where wilt thou flee?

4. Child of sin and sorrow, lift up thine
      eye!
Heirship thou canst borrow in worlds on
      high,
      In that high home,
      Graven thy name:
      Child of sin and sorrow,
      Swift homeward fly!

Trusting in Jesus.

C · C · G · C

1. Je - sus will nev - er, nev - er for - sake thee, When thou art
2. Down from on high he came to re - deem thee Left his bright
3. What tho' the dark - ness of gloom doth en - shroud thee, Blighting thy

D · G · D G · C · G

tempted O turn thou to him, Sin - ful al - lur-ments shall conquer thee
king-dom to suf-fer and die Now in thy weakness he ev - er is
hopes in the morning of life, Je - sus thy Day - Star is ris-ing to

C · C · C · G · C

nev - er, If from the Sav - ior a smile thou dost win, He with his
near thee, Smile in af - flic - tion, for Je - sus is nigh; He by his
cheer thee, He will dis - perse all the shades of the night; He by his

A · E · E · A B

blood has willing - ly bought thee Ev - er his strength to thy weakness will lend.
pow-er ev - er doth shield thee, And with thy sor - row will com-fort-ing blend.
love doth tender-ly draw thee, Mercy and grace he sure-ly will send.

Refrain.

Je - sus will nev-er, nev-er for-sake thee Trust in him always, he's ever thy Friend.

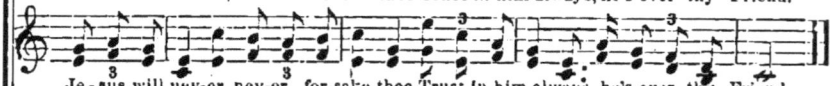

Je - sus will nev-er, nev-er for-sake thee Trust in him always, he's ever thy Friend.

Jubilate Deo.

DR. CROFT.

1. O be joyful in the Lord, | all ye | lands; ‖ Serve the Lord with gladness and come before his | presence | with a | song.
2. Be ye sure that the Lord | he is | God; ‖ It is he that hath made us, and not we ourselves, we are his people | and the | sheep..of his | pasture.
3. O go your way into his gates with thanksgiving and into his | courts with | praise; ‖ Be ye thankful unto him and speak | good.... | of his | Name.
4. For the Lord is gracious, his mercy is | ev-er- | lasting, ‖ And his truth endureth from gener- | ation..to | gen -- er- | ation.
5. Glory be to the Father, and | to the | Son, ‖ And | to the | Holy | Ghost.
6. As it was in the beginning, is now, and | ever..shall | be, ‖ World | without | end..A- | men.

The Lord is My Shepherd.

Tune.—"Flow Gently Sweet Afton," S. S. Bell No. 2—183, Key of A.

1. The Lord is my Shepherd, how happy am I !
How tender and watchful my wants to supply !
He daily provides me with raiment and food,
Whate'er he denies me is meant for my good.
The Lord is my Shepherd, then must I obey
His gracious commandment, and walk in his way—
His fear he will teach me, my heart he'll renew,
And tho' I'm so sinful, my sins he'll subdue.

2. The Lord is my Shepherd, how happy am I !
I'm blest while I live, and I'm blest when I die,
In death's gloomy valley no evil I'll dread,
" For I will be with thee," my Shepherd has said.
" The Lord is my Shepherd," I'll sing with delight,
Till called to adore him in regions of light;
Then praise him, with angels, to bright harps of gold,
And ever and ever his glory behold.

Around the Throne of God, &c.

S. S. BELL No. 1—44, Key of G ; also S. S. Hosanna 58, H. Voices 11, G. Chain 118.

1. Around the throne of God in heaven
Thousands of children stand,
Children whose sins are all forgiven,
A holy, happy band,
Singing glory, glory,
Glory be to God on high.

2. In flowing robes of spotless white
See every one array'd,
Dwelling in everlasting light,
And joys that never fade,
Singing glory, &c.

3. What brought them to that world above,
That heaven so bright and fair,
Where all is peace, and joy, and love ?
How came those children there ?
Singing glory, &c.

4. Because the Saviour shed his blood,
To wash away their sin ;
Bathed in that pure and precious flood,
Behold them white and clean !
Singing glory, &c.

5. On earth they sought the Saviour's grace,
On earth they loved his name ;
So now they see his blessed face,
And stand before the Lamb,
Singing glory, &c.

On this New Year Evening, &c.

Tune.—" Prairie Flower," Key of B flat.

1. On this New Year evening, when our hearts are light,
All around us cheerful, gay, and bright,
With our happy voices let us fill the air,
And a Father's love declare.
Merrily we sing, then, children, one and all,
Praise your bounteous Giver, great and small,
For the many mercies daily he bestows,
From the dawn till evening's close.
CHO.—Bright, happy New Year ! joyful we sing,
Hearts full of gladness now we bring ;
Take these offerings, Jesus, full of love and cheer,
Smile upon the glad New Year.

2. Come, dear children, join our happy little band,
Pressing onward to the " better land."
Where the angels welcome, with their harps of gold,
All the lambs of Jesus' fold.
In the land of sunshine sorrow is unknown
All is calm and peaceful round the throne;
Come ye sad and weary to this place of rest,
Come and be forever blest.
CHO.—Bright, happy New Year, &c.

Pilgrim Chorus.

MERRY CHIMES 143, Key of C.

From afar, gracious Lord, thou didst gather
Thy flock, on these shores of the ocean,
Thee they owned as their God and their Father ;
And when left in the wild waste forlorn,
Still they served thee, with steadfast devotion.
Hear the cry which their children are sending,
With the accents of penitence blending,
Save thy people from peril and scorn :
O, let peace bend its iris arch o'er us,
Gentle breezes and waves with our voices,
Sing of light, love and freedom in chorus,
Till the Eden of old be renewed.
Ah ! our sins would call down thy displeasure,
But thy goodness the sad heart rejoices,
Be thy mercy displayed without measure,
And by mercy our soul be subdued.

I Will Seek my Father.*

Reverentially.

From Blumenthal, by F. W. Root.

1. When the morn is bright and fair, When sweet songsters charm the air,
2. In the sol - i - tude a - part, In the wil - der - ness or mart,
3. When the ev'n - ing sun is red, When each blos - som droops its head,

I will lift my heart in prayer, I will seek my Fath - er.

Oh! my sore - ly tempt-ed heart, I will seek my Fath - er.
Kneel-ing low be - side my bed, I will seek my Fath - er:

Lest my feet should go a - stray From His pure and per - fect way;

In the dark-ness of the day, He shall be my guide and stay;
That I slum - ber in His care, Shield - ed from each harm - ful snare;

Lest I grieve Him as I may, I will seek my Fath - er.

I will lean on Him al - way: I will seek my Fath - er.
And for life and death pre - pare; I will seek my Fath - er.

*From Chapel Gems, by Permission of Root & Cady.

Sweet Land of Rest.

G. CENSER 13, Key of G; also Pil. Songs 90, Glad
                Tidings 84.

1. Sweet land of rest! for thee I sigh,
   When will the moment come
When I shall lay my armor by
   And dwell with Christ at home?
   CHO.—Home, home, sweet, sweet home,
          And dwell with Christ at home.

2. No tranquil joys on earth I know,
   No peaceful sheltering home;
This world's a wilderness of wo
   This world is not my home.
   CHO.—Home, home, &c.

3. To Jesus Christ I sought for rest,
   He bade me cease to roam,
But fly for succor to his breast,
   And he'd conduct me home.
   CHO.—Home, home, &c.

4. Weary of wandering round and round
   This vale of sin and gloom,
I long to leave the unhallow'd ground
   And dwell with Christ at home.
   CHO.—Home, home, &c.

Lonely Traveler.

G. CHAIN 65, Key of G; also Oriola 198, or S. S.
                Hosanna 107.

1. I'm a lonely traveler here,
   Weary, oppress'd;
But my journey's end is near,
   Soon I shall rest.
Dark and dreary is the way,
   Toiling I've come;
Ask me not with you to stay:
   Yonder's my home.

2. I'm a weary traveler here,
   I must go on;
For my journey's end is near,
   I must be gone.
Brighter joys than earth can give
   Win me away;
Pleasures that forever live:
   I cannot stay.

3. I'm a traveler to a land
   Where all is fair,
Where is seen no broken band:
   Saints all are there.
Where no tear shall ever fall,
   No heart be sad;
Where the glory is for all,
   And all are glad.

4. I'm a traveler, and I go
   Where all is fair:
Farewell, all I've loved below,
   I must be there.
Worldly honors, hopes, and gain,
   All I resign;

Welcome sorrow, grief, and pain,
   If heaven be mine.

5. I'm a traveler, call me not:
   Upward's my way;
Yonder is my rest and lot:
   I cannot stay.
Farewell, earthly pleasures all,
   Pilgrim I roam:
Hail me not; in vain you call:
   Yonder's my home.

Be Kind to the Loved Ones, &c.

S. S. BELL, No. 2—46, Key of A flat; or S. S.
                Hosanna 82.

1. Be kind to thy father; for when thou
                wast young,
   Who loved thee so fondly as he?
He caught the first accents that fell from
      thy tongue,
   And join'd in thy innocent glee.
Be kind to thy father, for now he is old,
   His locks intermingled with gray;
His footsteps are feeble,—once fearless
      and bold;
   Thy father is passing away.

2. Be kind to thy mother; for lo! on her
                brow
   May traces of sorrow be seen;
Oh, well mayst thou cherish and comfort
      her now,
   For loving and kind she hath been.
Remember thy mother; for thee will she
      pray
   As long as God giveth her breath;
With accents of kindness, then, cheer her
      lone way,
   E'en to the dark valley of death.

3. Be kind to thy brother: his heart will
                have dearth
   If the smile of thy joy be withdrawn;
The flowers of feeling will fade at their
      birth,
   If the dew of affection be gone.
Be kind to thy brother, wherever you are;
   The love of a brother shall be
An ornament purer and richer by far
   Than pearls from the depth of the sea.

4. Be kind to thy sister; not many may
                know
   The depth of true sisterly love;
The wealth of the ocean lies fathoms
      below
   The surface that sparkles above.   [bold,
Be kind to thy father, once fearless and
Be kind to thy mother so near;
Be kind to thy brother, nor show thy heart
      cold;
   Be kind to thy sister so dear.

W. Irving Hartshorn.

1. There are an - gels bend - ing low, Wait - ing for me to de - cide;
2. Will the lit - tle I can do, E'er en - sure such heav'n - ly gain;

Shall I serve the Lord, or no? Am I on the Sav - ior's side?
Will my feet e'er wan - der thro' Yon bright an - gel trod - den plain?

Yes, un - furl your snow - y wings, Bear this message to the skies,
Thou wilt guide me, Sav - ior, Friend, To the blest trans - port - ing scene,

I'll give up all less - er things, For the Lord of Par - a - dise.
To the joys that nev - er end, To the pas - tures ev - er green.

Refrain.

Yes, I'll bear the cross for thee, Yes, I'll bear the cross for thee,

rit, ad lib

Thou did'st die to ran - som me, Sin - less Lamb of Cal - va - ry.

Joyfully ! Joyfully !

H. Voices 211, Key of G ; also Oriola 121, S. S.
Bell No 1−51.

1. Joyfully, joyfully, onward we move,
Bound to the land of bright spirits above
Jesus, our Saviour, in mercy says, Come,
Joyfully, joyfully, haste to your home.
Soon will our pilgrimage end here below.
Soon to the presence of God we shall go ;
Then if to Jesus our hearts have been
given,
Joyfully, joyfully, rest we in heaven.

2. Teachers and scholars have pass'd on
before,
Waiting, they watch us approaching the
shore,
Singing to cheer us, while passing along,
Joyfully, joyfully, haste to your home.
Sounds of sweet music there ravish the
ear,
Harps of the blessed, your strains we shall
hear,
Filling with harmony heaven's high dome.
Joyfully, joyfully, Jesus, we come.

3. Death with his arrow may soon lay us
low,
Safe in our Saviour, we fear not the blow ;
Jesus hath broken the bars of the tomb,
Joyfully, joyfully, will we go home.
Bright will the morn of eternity dawn,
Death shall be conquer'd, his sceptre be
gone,
Over the plains of sweet Canaan we'll
roam
Joyfully, joyfully, safely at home.

The Mercy-Seat.

G. Shower 10, Key of E ; Pilgrims' Songs 4.

1. From ev'ry stormy wind that blows,
From ev'ry swelling tide of woes,
There is a calm, a sure retreat,
'Tis found beneath the Mercy-seat.
Cho.—The Mercy-seat, the Mercy-seat,
The blessed Mercy-seat,
The Mercy-seat, the Mercy-seat,
The blessed Mercy-seat.

2. There is a place where Jesus sheds
The oil of gladness on our heads,—
A place than all beside more sweet :
It is the blood-bought Mercy-seat.
Cho.—The Mercy-seat, &c.

3. There is a scene where spirits blend,
Where friend holds fellowship with friend;
Though sunder'd far, by faith they meet
Around one common Mercy-seat.
Cho.—The Mercy-seat, &c.

4. There, there on eagle wings we sour,
And sin and sense molest no more,
And heaven comes down our souls to
greet,
And glory crowns the Mercy-seat.
Cho.—The Mercy-seat, &c.

To-Day the Saviour Calls.

S. S. Hosanna 63, Key of F ; also H. Voices 79,
Oriola 61.

1. To-day the Saviour calls :
Ye wanderers, come !
O ye benighted souls,
Why longer roam ?

2. To-day the Saviour calls ;
For refuge fly ;
The storm of vengeance falls,
Ruin is nigh.

3. To-day the Saviour calls
Oh, listen now !
Within these sacred walls
To Jesus bow.

4. The Spirit calls to-day,
Yield to his power ;
Oh, grieve him not away !
'Tis mercy's hour.

A Year Again has Passed, &c.

S. S. Bell No. 1—11, Key of D.

1. A year again has passed away !
Time swiftly speeds along ;
We come again to praise and pray,
And sing our greeting song.
Chorus.—We come, we come, we come
with song to greet you,
We come, we come, we come with song
again.

2. We come the Saviour's name to praise,
To sing the wondrous love
Of Him who guards us all our days,
And guides to Heaven above.
Cho.—We come, we come, &c.

3. We'll sing of mercies daily given,
Through every passing year,
We'll sing the promises of Heaven
With voices loud and clear.
Cho.—We come, we come, &c.

4. We'll sing of many a happy hour
We've passed in Sunday school,
Where truth, like summer's genial show-
ers,
Extends its gracious rule.
Cho.—We come, we come, &c.

5. Our youthful hearts will gladly raise,
Our voices sweetly sing
A general song of grateful praise,
To Heaven's eternal King.
Cho.—We come, we come, &c.

Looking to Jesus.

Words by H. R. PALMER.

1. Yield not to temp-ta-tion, For weakness is sin, Each vict'ry will help us, Some oth-er to win, Fight manful-ly onward, Dark passions sub-due, Look ev-er to Je-sus, He'll car-ry you through.

2. Shun e-vil com-pan-ions, Bad language dis-dain, God's name hold in rev'rence Nor take it in vain, Be thoughtful and earnest, Kind-hearted and true, Look ev-er to Je-sus, He'll car-ry you through.

3. To him that o'er-com-eth God giv-eth a crown Thro' faith we shall conquer, Tho' of-ten cast down, He who is the Sa-vior Our strength will re-new, Look ev-er to Je-sus, He'll car-ry you through.

Refrain.

Ask the Savior to help you, Com-fort, strengthen and keep you,

Repeat pp ad lib.

He is will-ing to aid you, He will car-ry you through.

There's a Cry from Macedonia.

From Bradbury's Golden CENSER 112, Key of E flat. By permission.

1. There's a cry from Macedonia—Come and help us ;
The light of the gospel bring, O come !
Let us hear the joyful tidings of salvation,
We thirst for the living spring.
O ye heralds of the cross be up and doing
Remember the great command, Away !
Go ye forth and preach the word to ev'ry creature,
Proclaim it in ev'ry land.
    They shall gather from the East,
    They shall gather from the West,
    With the patriarchs of old,
    And the ransom'd shall return
    To the kingdoms of the blest
    With their harps and crowns of gold.
There's a cry from Macedonia—Come and help us ;
The light of the gospel bring, O come !
Let us hear the joyful tidings of salvation,
We thirst for the living spring.

2. O how beautiful their feet upon the mountains
The tidings of peace who bring, *Who bring*
To the nations of the earth who sit in darkness,
And tell them of Zion's king ;
Then ye heralds of the cross be up and doing,
Go work in your master's field, Away !
Sound the trumpet, sound the trumpet of salvation,
The Lord is your strength and shield.
    Let the distant isles be glad,
    Let them hail the Saviour's birth,
    And the news of pardon free,
    Till the knowledge of the truth
    Shall extend to all the earth,
    As the waters o'er the sea.
    There's a cry from Macedonia. &c.

3. Ye have listed in the army of the faithful
Like heroes the battle fight, Away !
There are foes on every hand that will assail you,
Then gird on your armor bright ;
With the banner of the cross unfurled before you,
The sword of the spirit wield, Away !
Ye shall conquer through his mercy who hath loved you,
The Lord is your strength and shield.
    Ye are marching to the land
    Where the saints in glory stand,
    And the just for joy shall sing,
    Ye by faith may bring it nigh ;
    Ye shall reach it bye and bye,
    And your shouts of triumph ring,
    There's a cry from Macedonia, &c.

Remember Thy Creator.

Tune.—"Children may come to the Saviour."
(See opposite page.)

1. Remember now thy Creator,
    In days of thy youth,
    Forget not his truth ;
O turn not away from thy Maker,
    His mercy invites you to-day.
    CHO.—Children may come, &c.

2. Remember now thy Creator,
    For dark day's will come,
    If in sin you shall roam,
In his law and his love there's no pleasure,
    For those who reject him to-day.
    CHO.—Children may come, &c.

3. Remember *now* thy Creator—
    Ere the silver cord loose,
    Or the golden bowl break,
Or the pitcher be broke at the fountain :
    Death lurks in the thought of delay.
    CHO.—Children may come, &c.
                            A. McLeish.

Jesus Loves Me.

G. SHOWER 68, Key of E flat ; also H. Voices 105, or Diadem 35.

1. Jesus loves me ! this I know,
For the Bible tells me so :
Little ones to him belong,
They are weak, but he is strong.
    CHO.—Yes, Jesus loves me,
        Yes, Jesus loves me,
        Yes, Jesus loves me,
        The Bible tells me so.

2. Jesus loves me ! He who died,
Heaven's gate to open wide ;
He will wash away my sin,
Let his little child come in.
    CHO.—Yes, Jesus loves me, &c.

3. Jesus loves me ! loves me still,
Though I'm very weak and ill ;
From his shining throne on high,
Comes to watch me where I lie.
    CHO.—Yes, Jesus loves me, &c.

4. Jesus loves me ! He will stay
Close beside me all the way :
If I love him, when I die
He will take me home on high.
    CHO.—Yes, Jesus loves me, &c.

Dismissal.

Tune.—"Sicilian Hymn," Key of D.

1. Lord dismiss us with thy blessing,
Be with us where'er we go ;
Keep us from thy laws transgressing,
Give us each thy love to know—
    O protect us !
    Ever guide us,
Bring us home to heaven at last.
                        R. W. Bridge.

Words and Music by H. R. PALMER.

1. Je - sus loves lit - tle chil - dren; He is their friend His aid He will lend,
2. Je - sus, now doth in - treat you, List to his voice Oh! hear and re - joice;
3. Je - sus now doth com - mand you, Do not de-lay Oh! haste to o - bey;

Like a shepherd he'll lead them; Come to him, chil-dren, to - day.
He is rea - dy to meet you, Lit - tle ones turn not a - way.
Dan-gers dark will sur-round you, If from your Sa - vior you stray.

Refrain.

Children may come, Children may come Children may come to the Sa-vior.

Children may come, Children may come Children may come to the Sa-vior.

Chil-dren may come Chil-dren may come Children may come and be saved.

Chil-dren may come Chil-dren may come Children may come and be saved.

Chil-dren may come Chil-dren may come Children may come and be saved.

The Shining Shore.

G. CHAIN 83. Key of G; also P. Songs 118, H.
Voices 200, G. Tidings 121.

1. My days are gliding swiftly by,
   And I, a pilgrim stranger,
Would not detain them as they fly,—
   Those hours of toil and danger.
CHO.—For, oh, we stand on Jordan's
   strand,
   Our friends are passing over,
And just before, the shining shore
   We may almost discover.

2. We'll gird our loins, my brethren dear,
   Our heavenly home discerning ;
Our absent Lord has left us word,
   Let every lamp be burning.
CHO.—For, oh, we stand on Jordan's, &c.

3. Should coming days be cold and dark,
   We need not cease our singing ;
That perfect rest naught can molest
   Where golden harps are ringing.
CHO.—For, oh, we stand on Jordan's, &c.

4. Let sorrow's rudest tempest blow,
   Each chord on earth to sever ;
Our King says, Come, and there's our
   home,
   Forever, oh, forever.
CHO.—For, oh, we stand on Jordan's, &c.

Oh ! Who's Like Jesus ?

S. S. BELL No. 1—55, Key of G.

1. Jesus, my all, to heaven is gone ;
He whom I fix my hopes upon :
His track I see, and I'll pursue
The narrow way, till him I view.
CHORUS.—Oh ! who's like Jesus who died
   on the tree ?
He died for you, he died for me,
He died to set poor sinners free,
Oh! who's like Jesus who died on the tree ?

2. The way the holy prophets went,
The road that leads from banishment ;
The King's highway of holiness
I'll go for all his paths are peace.
CHO.—Oh ! who's like Jesus, &c.

3. This is the way I long have sought,
And mourned because I found it not ;
My grief and burden long has been,
Because I was not saved from sin.
CHO.—Oh ! who's like Jesus, &c.

4. The more I strove against its power,
I felt its weight and guilt the more ;
Till late I heard my Saviour say :
" Come hither, soul, I AM THE WAY."
CHO.—Oh ! who's like Jesus, &c.

5. Lo ! glad I come, and thou blest Lamb,
Shalt take me to thee, whose I am ;

Nothing but sin have I to give,
Nothing but love shall, I receive.
CHO.—Oh ! who's like Jesus, &c

6. Then will I tell to sinners round,
What a dear Saviour I have found ;
I'll point to thy redeeming blood,
And say, " Behold the way to God."
   CHO.—Oh ! who's like Jesus, &c.

The Gospel Invitation.

Tune.—Marlow, Key of G.

1. The Saviour calls, let every ear
   Attend the heavenly sound ;
Ye doubting souls, dismiss your fear ;
   Hope smiles reviving round.

2. For every thirsty, longing heart,
   Here streams of bounty flow ;
And life and health and bliss impart,
   To banish mortal woe.

3. Here springs of sacred pleasure rise,
   To ease your every pain ;
Immortal fountain ! full supplies !
   Nor shall you thirst in vain.

4. Ye sinners come,—'tis mercy's voice ;
   That gracious voice obey ;
Mercy invites to heavenly joys,
   And can you yet delay ?

5. Dear Saviour, draw reluctant hearts ;
   To thee let sinners fly
And take the bliss thy love imparts,
   And drink, and never die.

Behold a Stranger at the Door.

TUNE IN ORIOLA 100, Key of A.

1. Behold a stranger at the door !
He gently knocks,—has knock'd before,—
Has waited long, is waiting still ;
You treat no other friend so ill.

2. Oh, lovely attitude !—he stands
With melting heart and loaded hands :
Oh, matchless kindness !—and he shows
This matchless kindness to his foes !

3. But will he prove a friend indeed ?
He will,—the very Friend you need :
The Friend of sinners,—yes, 'tis he,
With garments dyed on Calvary.

4. Rise, touch'd with gratitude divine,
Turn out his enemy and thine,—
That soul-destroying monster, sin,—
And let the heavenly Stranger in.

5. Admit him ere his anger burn ;
His feet departed ne'er return ;
Admit him, or the hour's at hand
You'll at his door rejected stand.

Jesus at the Door.

Words by Rev. E. Eggleston.　　　　　　　　　　　　　　H. R. Palmer.

1. Jesus' voice my name is calling, Seeks my heart to win; Hardened is my
2. Pa-tient-ly the Lord is wait-ing, Wait-ing at the door; Pierced for me the

heart with sin-ning, Shall I let him in? Shall I hear his ten-der plead-ing
hand that's knocking, Knocking evermore. Wide the door with joy I'll o-pen,

Can I tell him nay? Can I close the door up-on him, See him turn a-way?
Bid the Lord come in! In my heart for-ev-er dwell-ing, Cast-ing out my sin.

Refrain

Hark, I hear my Sa-vior gent-ly knock-ing, knock-ing— While with fear my
I will o-pen to his gen-tle knock-ing, knock-ing— While with joy my

guilt-y heart is throb-bing, throb-bing; Je-sus stands with-out it, gent-ly
glad-den'd heart is throb-bing, throb-bing; Je-sus stands with-out, no long-er

Slower.

knock-ing, knock-ing— Christ, my Sa-vior, knock-ing at the door.
knock-ing, knock-ing— Christ, my Sa-vior, en-ters at the door.

Watchman, Tell us, &c.

S. S. BELL No. 1—90, Key of D.

1. Watchman, tell us of the night,
What its signs of promise are,
Traveler, o'er yon mountain's height,
See that glory beaming star !
Watchman, does its beauteous ray
Aught of hope or joy foretell ?
Traveler, yes ; it brings the day :
Promised day of Israel.
CHO.—Traveler, yes ; it brings the day—
Promised day of Israel !

2. Watchman, tell us of the night,
Higher yet that star ascends ;
Traveler, blessedness and light,
Peace and truth its course portends ;
Watchman, will its beams alone
Gild the spot that gave them birth ?
Traveler, ages are its own :
See, it bursts o'er all the earth !
CHO.—Traveler, ages are its own :
See, it bursts o'er all the earth !

3. Watchman, tell us of the night,
For the darkness seems to dawn,
Traveler, darkness takes its flight,
Doubt and terror are withdrawn.
Watchman, let thy wanderings cease ;
Hie thee to thy quiet home :—
Traveler, lo ! the Prince of Peace,
Lo ! the Son of God is come !
CHO.—Traveler, lo ! the Prince of Peace,
Lo, the Son of God is come,

I Would not Live Alway !

S. S. BELL No. 1—108, Key of F.

1. I would not live alway ! I ask not to
stay
Where storm after storm rises dark o'er
the way ;
The few lurid mornings that dawn on us
here
Are enough for life's woes—full enough
for its cheer.

2. I would not live alway ! thus fettered
by sin !
Temptation without, and corruption within !
E'en the rapture of pardon is mingled
with fears,
And the cup of thanksgiving with penitent tears.

3. I would not live alway ! no, welcome
the tomb !
Since Jesus hath lain there I dread not its
gloom ;
There sweet be my rest till he bid me
arise,

To hail him in triumph descending the
skies.

4. Who, who would live alway, away from
his God—
Away from yon heaven, that blissful abode,
Where the rivers of pleasure flow o'er the
bright plains,
And the noontide of glory eternally reigns.

5. Where the saints of all ages in harmony meet,
Their Saviour and brethren transported
to greet,
While the anthems of rapture unceasing-
ly roll,
And the smile of the Lord is the feast of
the soul !

Homeward Bound.

S. S. BELL No. 1.—64, Key of A ; Oriola 22, S
S. Hosanna 42, Happy Voices 210,

1. Out on an ocean all boundless we ride,
We're homeward bound ;
Toss'd on the waves of a rough, restless
tide.
We're homeward bound ;
Far from the safe quiet harbor we've rode,
Seeking our Father's celestial abode,
Promise of which on us each he bestowe'd:
We're homeward bound.

2. Wildly the storm sweeps us on as it
roars.
We're homeward bound.
Look ! yonder lie the bright heavenly
shores,
We're homeward bound ;
Steady, O pilot ! stand firm at the wheel ;
Steady ! we soon shall outweather the
gale.
Oh, how we fly 'neath the loud creaking
sail !
We're homeward bound.

3. We'll tell the world, as we journey
along,
We're homeward bound ;
Try to persuade them to enter our throng,
We're homeward bound.
Come, trembling sinner, forlorn and op-
press'd,
Join in our number, oh, come and be blest,
Journey with us to the mansions of rest ;
We're homeward bound.

4. Into the harbor of heaven we glide,
We're home at last ;
Softly we drift on its bright silver tide,
We're home at last ;
Glory to God ! all our dangers are o'er,
We stand secure on the glorified shore.
Glory to God ! we will shout evermore.
We're home at last.

If I would be an Angel.

H. R. PALMER.

Solo.

1. If I would be an an - gel, And with the angels stand, And sing the Savior's
2. He says that I must love him With mind, and heart, and soul, That ev'ry tho't and
3. He pro - mises to keep me, In ev'-ry try-ing hour, Of sorrow, sin, or

Duett.

prai - ses, In yon-der hap-py land— I must o-bey his precepts, Which
ac - tion Must yield to his con-trol; That if I hum-bly seek him, He'll
dan - ger, If I but trust his pow'r; And when this life is o - ver, He'll

he has kind-ly giv'n, To guide our wand'ring footsteps Unto the path of Heav'n.
pardon ev'-ry sin, And by his grace will help me, E-ter-nal life to win.
take me as his own, To stand among the an-gels, Be-fore his Father's throne.

Refrain.

Then I shall be an an-gel, And with the an-gels stand,

Then I shall be an an-gel, And with the an-gels stand,

A crown up-on my fore-head, A harp with-in my hand.

A crown up-on my fore-head, A harp with-in my hand.

I'm a Pilgrim.

S. S. BELL, No. 1—26, Key of G; also S. S. Hosanna, 43, Oriola, 127.

1. I'm a pilgrim, and I'm a stranger ;
I can tarry, I can tarry but a night.
Do not detain me, for I am going
To where the fountains are ever flowing.
I'm a pilgrim, and I'm a stranger,
I can tarry, I can tarry but a night.

2. There the glory is ever shining :
I am longing, I am longing for the sight.
Here in this country so dark and dreary
I have been wandering, forlorn and weary.
CHORUS.—I'm a pilgrim, &c.

3. There's the city to which I journey
My Redeemer, my Redeemer is its light ;
There is no sorrow, nor any sighing,
There is no sin there, nor any dying.
CHORUS.—I'm a pilgrim, &c.

Rest for the Weary.

G. CHAIN 36, Key of C; also S. S. Hosanna, 61, Pilgrims' Songs 56.

1. In the Christian's home in glory
There remains a land of rest ;
There my Saviour's gone before me,
To fulfil my soul's request.
‖: There is rest for the weary, :‖
There is rest for you,
On the other side of Jordan,
In the sweet fields of Eden,
Where the tree of life is blooming,
There is rest for you.

2. He is fitting up my mansion,
Which eternally shall stand ;
For my stay shall not be transient
In that holy, happy land.
CHORUS.—There is rest, &c.

3. Pain and sickness ne'er shall enter,
Grief nor woe my lot shall share,
But in that celestial centre
I a crown of life shall wear.
CHORUS.—There is rest, &c.

4. Sing, oh, sing, ye heirs of glory ;
Shout your triumphs as you go ;
Zion's gates will open for you,
You will find an entrance through.
CHORUS.—There is rest, &c.

Happy Day.

S. S. BELL No. 1—41, Key of G; also S. S. Hosanna 77, Happy Voices 43, Oriola 206,

1. Preserved by thine almighty power,
O Lord, our Maker, Saviour, King,
And brought to see this happy hour,
We come thy praises here to sing.
CHORUS.—Happy day, happy day !

Here in thy courts we'll gladly stay,
And at thy footstool humbly pray
That thou wouldst take our sins away.
Happy day, happy day,
When Christ shall wash our sins away !

2. We praise thee for thy constant care,
For life preserved, for mercies given :
Oh, may we still those mercies share,
And taste the joys of sins forgiven !
CHORUS.—Happy day, &c.

3. We praise thee for the joyful news
Of pardon through a Saviour's blood ;
O Lord, incline our hearts to choose
The way to happiness and God.
CHORUS.—Happy day, &c.

4. And when on earth our days are done,
Grant, Lord, that we at length may join,
Teachers and scholars, round thy throne,
The song of Moses and the lamb.
CHORUS.—Happy day, &c.

I Was a Wandering Sheep.

S. S. BELL No. 1 8, Key of F ; also H. Voices 45, or S. S. Hosanna 145.

1. I was a wandering sheep,
I did not love the fold ;
I did not love my Shepherd's voice,
I would not be controll'd ;
I was a wayward child,
I did not love my home,
I did not love my Father's voice,
I loved afar to roam.

2. The Shepherd sought his sheep,
The Father sought his child ;
They follow'd me o'er vale and hill
O'er deserts waste and wild :
They found me nigh to death,
Famish'd and faint and lone ;
They bound me with the bands of love,
They saved the wandering one.

3. Jesus my Shepherd is ;
'Twas he that loved my soul,
'Twas he that washed me in his blood,
'Twas he that made me whole :
'Twas he that sought the lost,
That found the wandering sheep ;
'Twas he that brought me to the fold ;
'Tis he that still doth keep.

4. No more a wandering sheep,
I love to be controll'd ;
I love my tender Shepherd's voice,
I love the peaceful fold.
No more a wayward child,
I seek no more to roam
I love my heavenly Father's voice ;
I love, I love his home.

Jesus said of little Children.

For Infant Classes.　J. A. BUTTERFIELD.

Je - sus said of lit - tle chil - dren,　Je - sus said of lit - tle chil - dren,
O! we love thee blessed Sav - ior,　O! we love thee, blessed Sav - ior,

Je - sus said of lit - tle chil - dren, Suf - fer them to come to me;
O! we love thee, blessed Sav - ior, And we want to go to thee;

Refrain.

Sing-ing, singing with the an - gels, Sing-ing, singing with the an - gels,

Sing-ing, singing with the an - gels, Hal - le - lu - jah, Praise the Lord.

2. :‖:We shall see the tree of heaven :‖:
With the leaves of healing balm,
:‖:And shall hear the angels singing,:‖:
Hallelujah to the Lamb.

3. :‖:We shall wander by the river, :‖:
Of everlasting life,
:‖:Where no sin can come forever,:‖:
With its sorrow and its strife.

List thy Bosom's door.

H. R. PALMER.

1. In the silent midnight watches | List thy bosom's door,‖
How it knocketh, knocketh, knocketh. | knocketh evermore!
2. Say not 'tis thy pulses beating. | 'Tis thy heart of sin;‖
'Tis thy Savior knocks, and crieth. | "Rise and let me in!"
3. Death comes down with reckless footsteps. | To the hall and hut;‖
Think you death will tarry knocking, | When the door is shut?
4. Jesus waiteth, waiteth, waiteth. | But the door is fast;‖
Grieved, away the Savior goeth, | Death breaks in at last,
5. Then 'tis time to stand entreating | Christ to let you in;‖
At the gate of heaven beating, | Wailing for thy sin.
6. Nay! alas, thou guilty creature! | Hast thou then forgot?‖
Jesus waited long to know thee, | Now he knows thee not.

Guide Me, O Thou, &c.

S. S. HOSANNA 128, Key of D; also H. Voices 69, Oriola 200.

1. Guide me, O thou great Jehovah,
Pilgrim through this barren land ;
I am weak, but thou art mighty ;
Hold me with thy powerful hand :
Bread of heaven,
Feed me till I want no more.

2. Open thou the crystal fountain
Whence the healing waters flow ;
Let the fiery, cloudy pillar
Lead me all my journey through :
Strong Deliverer,
Be thou still my strength and shield.

3. When I tread the verge of Jordan,
Bid the swelling stream divide ;
Death of death, and hell's destruction,
Land me safe on Canaan's side ;
Songs of praises
I will ever give to thee.

How Serious Is, &c.

Tune.--·Boylston, Key of C.

1. How serious is the charge
To train the infant mind !
'Tis God alone must give the heart,
To such a work inclined.

2. May we, in Christian bonds,
The Christian name adorn
By active deeds for public good,
Nor mind the sinner's scorn.

3. While wicked men unite,
Our youth to lead aside,
'Tis ours to show them wisdom's path,
In wisdom's path to guide.

4. Dependent, Lord, on thee
Our humble means to bless,
We gladly join our hearts and hands
And look for large success.

Rock of Ages.

S. S. HOSANNA, 33, Key of C; also H. Voices 182.

1. Rock of Ages, cleft for me !
Let me hide myself in thee ;
Let the water and the blood,
From thy wounded side that flow'd,
Be of sin the perfect cure ;
Save me, Lord, and make me pure.

2. Should my tears forever flow,
Should my zeal no languor know,
This for sin could not atone ;
Thou must save, and thou alone :
In my hand no price I bring,
Simply to thy cross I cling.

3. While I draw this fleeting breath,
When mine eyelids close in death,
When I rise to worlds unknown,

And behold thee on thy throne,
Rock of Ages, cleft for me,
Let me hide myself in thee !

Now Condescend, &c.

EVAN, Key of A flat; also G. Censer 93, S. S. Hosanna 3.

1. Now condescend, Almighty King,
To bless this happy throng ;
And kindly listen while we sing
Our grateful morning song.

2. We come to own the power divine
That watches o'er our days ;
For this our cheerful voices join
In hymns of grateful praise.

3. We come to learn thy holy word
And ask thy tender care ;
Before thy throne, Almighty Lord,
We bend in humble prayer.

4. May we in safety pass this day,
From sin and danger free ;
And ever walk in that sure way
That leads to heaven and thee. .

Nearer, My God, to Thee.

S. S. HOSANNA, Key of G.

1. Nearer, my God, to thee,
Nearer to thee :
E'en though it be a cross
That raiseth me.
Still all my song shall be,
Nearer, my God, to thee,
Nearer my God, to thee,
Nearer to thee.

2. Though like a wanderer,
Daylight all gone,
Darkness be over me,
My rest a stone,
Yet in my dreams I'd be
Nearer, my God, &c.

3. There let the way appear
Steps up to heaven ;
All that thou sendest me
In mercy given,
Angels to beckon me
Nearer, my God, &c.

4. Then, with my waking thoughts
Bright with thy praise,
Out of my stony griefs
Bethel I'll raise,
So by my woes to be
Nearer my God, &c.

5. Or if, on joyful wing
Cleaving the sky,
Sun, moon, and stars forgot,
Upward I fly,
Still all my song shall be,
Nearer, my God, &c.

Beautiful City.

Composed by request, for the Sunday School of H. W. Beecher's Church.

T. J. Cook.

1. Beautiful Zi - on, built a - bove, Beautiful cit - y that I love;
2. Beautiful heav'n where all is light, Beautiful an - gels, clothed in white;

8. Beautiful crowns on ev - ery brow, Beautiful palms the conq'erors show;
4. Beautiful throne for Christ our King, Beautiful songs the an - gels sing;

Beautiful gates of pearl - y white, Beautiful tem - ple—God its light!
Beautiful strains that nev - er tire, Beautiful harps thro' all the choir;

Beautiful robes the ransom'd wear, Beautiful all who en - ter there;
Beautiful rest— all wand'rings cease, Beautiful home of per - fect peace;

He who was slain on Cal - va - ry, Opens those pear-ly gates to me.
There shall I join the cho - rus sweet, Worship-ing at the Saviour's feet.

Thither I press with ea - ger feet, There shall my rest be long and sweet.
There shall my eyes the Sa - viour see, Haste to His heavenly home with me.

Refrain.　　　　　　　　　　　　　　　　　　　*Repeat pp*

Zi - on, Zi - on, love - ly Zi - on, Beau-ti-ful Zi - on, cit-y of our God.

Zi - on, Zi - on, love - ly Zi - on, Beau - ti-ful Zi - on, cit-y of our God.

*From "Now Olive Branch," by Permission of F. J. Huntington & Co.

When I Can Read, &c.

Tune.—"Ortonville," Key of B flat.

1. When I can read my title clear
To mansions in the skies,
I'll bid farewell to every fear,
And wipe my weeping eyes.

2. Should earth against my soul engage,
And fiery darts be hurl'd,
Then I can smile at Satan's rage,
And face a frowning world.

3. Let cares like a wild deluge come,
Let storms of sorrow fall,—
So I but safely reach my home,
My God, my heaven, my all.

4. There I shall bathe my weary soul
In seas of heavenly rest,
And not a wave of trouble roll
Across my peaceful breast.

Coronation.

G. Shower 53, Key of G ; also S. S. Hosanna 142,
or Diadem 3.

1. All hail the power of Jesus' name !
Let angels prostrate fall ;
Bring forth the royal diadem,
And crown him Lord of all.

2. Crown him, ye martyrs of our God,
Who from his altar call ;
Extol the stem of Jesse's rod,
And crown him Lord of all.

3. Ye chosen seed of Israel's race,
Ye ransom'd from the fall,
Hail him who saves you by his grace,
And crown him Lord of all.

4. Sinners, whose love can ne'er forget
The wormwood and the gall,
Go, spread your trophies at his feet,
And crown him Lord of all.

5. Let every kindred, every tribe,
On this terrestrial ball,
To him all majesty ascribe,
And crown him Lord of all,

Just as I Am.

Fresh Laurels 140, Key of E flat ; also G.
Showers 56, H. Voices 35.

1. Just as I am, without one plea,
But that thy blood was | shed for | me,
And that thou bid'st me | come to | thee,
O | Lamb of | God, I | come !

2. Just as I am, and waiting not
To rid my soul of | one dark | blot,
To thee, whose blood can | cleanse each |
spot,
O | Lamb of | God, I | come !

3. Just as I am, though toss'd about
With many a conflict, | many a | doubt,
Fightings within, and | foes with- | out,
O | Lamb of | God, I | come !

4. Just as I am, poor, wretched, blind,—
Sight, riches, healing | of the | mind,
Yea, all I need, in | thee I | find,—
O | Lamb of | God, I | come !

5. Just as I am,—thou wilt receive,
Wilt welcome, pardon, | cleanse, re | lieve
Because thy promise | I be- | lieve,—
O | Lamb of | God, I | come !

6. Just as I am, thy love, I own,
Has broken every | barrier | down ;
Now to be thine, and | thine a- | lone.
O | Lamb of | God, I | come !

Hymn for Palm Sunday.

Tune.—" Battle Hymn of the Republic," Key of
B flat.

1. When our beloved Jesus rode into Je-
rusalem,
Little children of the kingdom were
among the multitude.
Oh ! how lovingly he saw them, and how
sweetly smiled on them,
As their sweet voices rang,
Chorus.—Sing Hosanna in the highest !
Blessed, blessed be the king that cometh !
Blessed be the king that cometh !
In the name of the Lord !

2. As all along the path they strewed the
green and shining Palm,
Gentle hands of little children spread
the branches in the way
They were singing and rejoicing in a glad
and solemn psalm,
As their young voices rang,
Cho.—Sing Hosanna, &c.

3. And now the blessed Jesus has ascend-
ed up above ;
He has gone up from the olden, to the
new Jerusalem.
Now he looks down on the children, smi-
ling on them still, in love,
As their young voices sing,
Cho. Sing Hosanna, &c.

4. And by and by the children, who to fol-
low him will try,
Up to yonder heavenly city with the
pearly gates, shall go.
They shall go to cast their palms down,
in the golden street on high,
As their young voices ring,
Cho.—Sing Hosanna, &c.
Mary B. C. Slade.

Slow.

From an adaptation by W. LUDDEN.

1. When gathering clouds around I view, And days are dark, and friends are few,
2. If aught should tempt my soul to stray From heav'nly wis-dom's nar-row way,
3. When vex - ing tho'ts with-in me rise, And, sore dis-may'd, my spir - it dies;

4. When sorrowing o'er some stone I bend, Which cov-ers all that was a friend,
5. And, oh, when I have safe - ly past, Thro' ev'- ry con - flict but the last,

On Him I lean, who, not in vain, Experienced ev'- ry hu - man pain
To fly the good I would pur-sue, Or do the ill I would not do;
Then He, who once vouchsaf'd to bear The sick'ning an - guish of des - pair

And from his voice, his hand, his smile, Di-vides me for a lit - tle while;
Still, still un-chang-ing watch be-side My bed of death, for Thou has died;

He feels my griefs, he sees my fears, And counts and treasures up my tears.
Still He, who felt tempta - tion's pow'r, Shall guard me in that dang'rous hour.
Shall sweet-ly soothe,shall gen-tly dry, The throbbing heart, the streaming eye.

Thou Sav - ior, seest the tears I shed, For thou did'st weep o'er Lazarus dead.
Then point to realms of end - less day, And wipe the lat - est tear a - way.

Gloria Patri.

TALLIS.

Glory be to the Father, and | to the | Son, | and | to the | Holy Ghost,
As it was in the begining, is now, and | ever shall | be, | World with | out end. | A | men.

Jesus, Lover of my Soul.

Tune.--Martyn, Key of F.

1. Jesus, lover of my soul,
Let me to thy bosom fly,
While the raging billows roll,
While the tempest still is high ;
Hide me, O my Saviour hide,
Till the storm of life is past :
Safe into the haven guide,
Oh, receive my soul at last.

2. Other refuge have I none ;
Hangs my helpless soul on thee :
Leave, oh, leave me not alone !
Still support and comfort me.
All my trust on thee is stay'd ;
All my help from thee I bring ;
Cover my defenceless head
With the shadow of thy wing.

3. Thou, O Christ, art all I want ;
More than all in thee I find ;
Raise the fallen, cheer the faint,
Heal the sick, and lead the blind.
Just and holy is thy name,
I am all unrighteousness
False and full of sin I am,
Thou art full of truth and grace.

A Poor Wayfaring Man, &c.

ORIOLA 100, Key of A.

1. A poor wayfaring man of grief
Hath often cross'd me on my way,
Who sued so humbly for relief
That I could never answer nay.
I had not power to ask his name,
Wither he went, or whence he came ;
Yet there was something in his eye
That won my love, I knew not why.

2. Once, when my scanty meal was spread,
He enter'd ; not a word he spake
Just perishing for want of bread ;
I gave him all ; he bless'd it, brake,
And ate, but gave me part again.
Mine was an angel's portion then ;
And while I fed with eager haste,
The crust was manna to my taste.

3. I spied him where a fountain burst
Clear from the rock ; his strength was
gone ;
The heedless water mock'd his thirst ;
He heard it, saw it hurrying on.
I ran and raised the sufferer up ;
Thrice from the stream he drain'd my cup ;
Dipp'd, and return'd it running o'er ;
I drank, and never thirsted more.

4. 'Twas night ; the floods were out ; it
blew
A wintry hurricane aloof :
I heard his voice abroad, and flew

To bid him welcome to my roof.
I warm'd, I clothed, I cheer'd my guest,
Laid him on my own couch to rest,
Then made the earth my bed, and seem'd
In Eden's garden while I dream'd.

5. Then, in a moment, to my view
The stranger started from disguise ;
The tokens in his hands I knew ;
My Saviour stood before my eyes !
He spake, and my poor name he named :
"Of me thou hast not been ashamed ;
These deeds shall thy memorial be ;
Fear not ; thou didst it unto me."

Alas! and Did, &c.

Tune.—Balerma, Key of B flat.

1. Alas ! and did my Saviour bleed ?
And did my Sovereign die ?
Would he devote that sacred head
For such a worm as I ?

2. Was it for crimes that I had done
He groan'd upon the tree ?
Amazing pity ! grace unknown !
And love beyond degree !

3. Well might the sun in darkness hide,
And shut his glories in,
When God, the mighty Maker died
For man, the creature's sin.

4. Thus might I hide my blushing face
While his dear cross appears,
Dissolve my heart in thankfulness,
And melt mine eyes to tears.

5. But drops of grief can ne'er repay
The debt of love I owe :
Here, Lord, I give myself away ;
'Tis all that I can do.

Lord I Would Own, &c.

Tune.—Ortonville, Key of B flat.

1. Lord, I would own thy tender care,
And all thy love to me ;
The food I eat, the clothes I wear,
Are all bestow'd by thee.

2. And thou preservest me from death,
And dangers every hour ;
I cannot draw another breath
Unless thou give the power.

3. My health and friends and parents dear
To me by God are given ;
I have not any blessings here
But what are sent from heaven.

4. Such goodness, Lord, and constant care,
A child can ne'er repay ;
But may it be my daily prayer
To love thee and obey

Jesus is Mine.

1. Fade, fade each earthly joy, Je-sus is mine; Break every ten-der tie,
2. Tempt not my soul a-way, Je-sus is mine; Here would I ev-er stay,

3. Fare-well, ye dreams of night, Je-sus is mine; Lost in this dawning light,
4. Fare-well, mor-tal-i-ty, Je-sus is mine; Wel-come, e-ter-ni-ty,

Je-sus is mine; Dark is the wil-der-ness, Earth has no rest-ing-place,
Je-sus is mine; Per-ish-ing things of clay, Born but for one brief day,

Je-sus is mine; All that my soul has tried, Left but a dis-mal void
Je-sus is mine; Welcome, O lov'd and blest, Welcome, sweet scenes of rest,

For last stanza.

Je-sus a-lone can bless, Je-sus is mine;
Pass from my heart a-way, Je-sus is mine,

Je-sus has sat-is-fied, Je-sus is mine.
Welcome, my Sa-vior's breast, Je-sus is mine. A - - men.

The Lord's Prayer.

Our Father who art in heaven } hallowed.......... { be thy name { Thy kingdom come, thy will be done, on } earth, as it is in heaven,

Give us this day our.......... daily bread, { And forgive us our tres- } passes as we forgive.. { those who trespass a- [gainst us,

And lead us not into tempta- } tion, but deliver............ { us from evil, { For thine is the King- dom, and the power, and the glory, for - } ever and ever, A-men.

O Turn Ye, &c.

Tune.—Expostulation, Key of G.

1. Oh, turn ye, oh, turn ye, for why will
ye die,
When God in great mercy is coming so
nigh?
Now Jesus invites you, the Spirit says,
Come,
And angels are waiting to welcome you
home.

2. How vain the delusion, that while you
delay
Your hearts may grow better by staying
away!
Come wretched, come starving, come just
as you be,
While streams of salvation are flowing so
free.

3. And now Christ is ready your souls to
receive:
Oh, how can you question if you will believe?
If sin is your burden, why will you not
come?
'Tis you he bids welcome; he bids you
come home.

4. Come, give us your hand, and the Saviour your heart,
And, trusting in Heaven, we never shall
part;
Oh, how can we leave you? why will you
not come?
We'll journey together, and soon be at
home.

Psalm of Life.

Tune.—Autumn, Key of A flat

1. Tell me not in mournful numbers
"Life is but an empty dream!"
For the soul is dead that slumbers,
And things are not what they seem.
Life is real! life is earnest!
And the grave is not its goal;
"Dust thou art, to dust returnest,"
Was not spoken of the soul.

2. Art is long, and Time is fleeting,
And our hearts, though stout and brave,
Still, like muffled drums, are beating
Funeral marches to the grave.
In the world's broad field of battle,
In the bivouac of life,
Be not like dumb-driven cattle!
Be a hero in the strife!

3. Lives of great men all remind us
We can make our lives sublime,
And, departing, leave behind us
Foot-prints on the sands of time;

Foot-prints, that perhaps another,
Sailing o'er life's solemn main
A forlorn and shipwrecked brother,
Seeing, shall take heart again.

4. Not enjoyment, and not sorrow,
Is our destined end or way;
But to act, that each to-morrow
Finds us farther than to-day.
Let us, then, be up and doing,
With a heart for any fate;
Still achieving, still pursuing,
Learn to labor and to wait.

Welcome News.

Tune.—Zion, Key of D.

1. On the mountain's top appearing,
Lo, the sacred herald stands,
Welcome news to Zion bearing,
Zion long in hostile lands:
‖: Mourning captive,
God himself will loose thy bands. :‖

2. Has thy night been long and mournful?
Have thy friends unfaithful proved?
Have thy foes been proud and scornful,
By thy sighs and tears unmoved?
‖: Cease thy mourning!
Zion still is well beloved. :‖

3. God, thy God, will now restore thee;
He himself appears thy Friend;
All thy foes shall flee before thee;
Here their boasts and triumphs end.
‖: Great deliverance,
Zion's King vouchsafes to send. :‖

I Do Believe.

Tune.—The Sunday School.—G Chain 4, Key of
G; also Happy Voices 96.

1. How sweet the name of Jesus sounds
In a believer's ear!
It soothes his sorrows, heals his wounds,
And drives away his fear.
CHORUS.—I do believe, I now believe
That Jesus died for me,
And through his blood, his
precious blood,
I shall from sin be free.

2. It makes the wounded spirit whole,
And calms the troubled breast;
'Tis manna to the hungry soul,
And to the weary, rest.
CHORUS.—I do believe, &c.

3. Weak is the effort of my heart,
And cold my warmest thought;
But when I see thee as thou art,
I'll praise thee as I ought,
CHORUS.—I do believe, &c.

H. R. PALMER.

1. Sing of Je - sus sing for - ev - er, Of the love that chang-es nev - er,

2. Pa - tient-ly and per - se - ver-ing, Let us la - bor nev - er fear-ing,

3. Though we pass through trib-u - la - tion, Christ will be our con - so - la - tion

Who, or what from him can sev - er Those he makes his own!

While we wait for his ap - pear-ing, All will then be well,

Ours will be a full sal - va - tion, All will then be well,

With his blood the Lord hath bought us, When we knew him not he sought us,

By his word his fears al - lay - ing, All our fee - ble foot-steps stay-ing,

Hap-py still in God con - fid - ing, Fruit-ful if in Christ a - bid - ing;

And from all our wonderings brought us, His the praise a - lone.

Let us nev - er cease our pray-ing, All will then be well.

Ho - ly through the spir - it's guid-ing, Wo with Him will dwell.

O'er the Gloomy Hills, &c.

Tune.--"Zion," Key of D.

1. O'er the gloomy hills of darkness,
Cheer'd by no celestial ray,
Sun of Righteousness, arising,
Bring the bright, the glorious day ;
‖:Send the gospel
To the earth's remotest bound.:‖

2. Kingdoms wide that sit in darkness—
Grant them, Lord, the glorious light,
And from eastern coast to western
May the moring chase the night,
‖:And redemption,
Freely purchased, win the day.:‖

3. Fly abroad, thou mighty gospel !
Win and conquer, never cease ;
May thy lasting, wide dominions
Multiply and still increase ;
‖:Sway thy scepter,
Saviour, all the world around.:‖

From Greenland's Icy Mountains.

ORIOLA 174, Key of E ; also S. S. Hosanna 119,
H. Voices 125.

1. From Greenland's icy mountains.
From India's coral strand ;
Where Afric's sunny fountains
Roll down their golden sand ;
From many an ancient river,
From many a palmy plain,—
They call us to deliver
Their land from error's chain.

2. What though the spicy breezes
Blow soft o'er Ceylon isle,
Though every prospect pleases,
And only man is vile ?
In vain with lavish kindness
The gifts of God are strewn ;
The heathen, in his blindness,
Bows down to wood and stone.

3. Shall we, whose souls are lighted
With wisdom from on high,
Shall we to men benighted
The lamp of life deny ?
Salvation ! Oh, salvation !
The joyful sound proclaim,
Till earth's remotest nation
Has learn'd Messiah's name.

4. Waft, waft, ye winds, his story,
And you, ye waters, roll,
Till, like a sea of glory,
It spread from pole to pole ;
Till o'er our ransom'd nature
The Lamb for sinners slain,
Redeemer, King, Creator,
In bliss returns to reign.

The Morning Light is Breaking.

Tune.—Webb, Key of B flat.

1. The morning light is breaking,
The darkness disappears,
The sons of earth are waking
To penitential tears :
Each breeze that sweeps the ocean
Brings tidings from afar
Of nations in commotion,
Prepared for Zion's war.

2. Rich dews of grace come o'er us
In many a gentle shower,
And brighter scenes before us
Are opening every hour ;
Each cry to heaven going
Abundant answer brings,
And heavenly gales are blowing
With peace upon their wings.

3. See heathen nations bending
Before the God we love
And thousands heart ascending
In gratitude and love ;
While sinners, now confessing,
The gospel call obey,
And seek the Saviour's blessing,—
A nation in a day.

4. Blest river of salvation,
Pursue thine onward way,
Flow thou to every nation,
Nor in thy richness stay ;
Stay not, till all the lowly
Triumphant reach their home ;
Stay not, till all the holy
Proclaim, "The Lord is come."

The Lord is my Shepherd.

SILVER CHIMES 89, Key of D.

1. The Lord is my Shepherd, I | shall not | want ;‖ He maketh me to lie down in green pastures ; He leadeth me be- | side the | still— | waters.

2. He restoreth my soul ; He leadeth me in the paths of righteousness for his | name's— | sake.‖ Yea, though I walk through the valley of the shadow of death, I will fear no evil, for thou art with me, thy rod and thy | staff, they | comfort | me.

3. Thou preparest a table before me in the presence of mine enemies ; Thou anointest my head with oil, my | cup runneth | over,‖ Surely goodness and mercy shall follow me all the days of my life, and I shall dwell in the | house of the | Lord for- | ever. | Amen.

Shall we meet beyond the River.

H. R. PALMER.

1. Shall we meet be - yond the Riv - er, Where the sur - ges cease to roll,
2. Shall we meet in that blest har - bor, When our storm - y voyage is o'er,
3. Where the mu - sic of the ran-som'd Rolls in har - mo-ny a - round,
4. Shall we meet with many a lov'd one, Torn on earth from our em - brace?
5. Shall we meet with Christ our Sa - vior When he comes to claim his own?

Where, in all the bright for-ev - er, Sor - row ne'er shall press the soul?
Shall we meet and cast the an - chor By the fair ce - les - tial shore?
And cre - a - tion swells the cho - rus With its sweet me-lo-dious sound?
Shall we lis - ten to their voi - ces, And be - hold them face to face?
Shall we hear him bid us wel - come, And sit down up-on his throne?

Refrain.

Yes, we'll meet, yes, we'll meet, Where the surges cease to roll,

Yes, we'll meet, yes, we'll meet, Where the sur - ges cease to roll,

Yes, we'll meet, yes, we'll meet,

Yes, we'll meet be - yond the riv - er, Where the sur - ges cease to roll.

Yes, we'll meet be - yond the riv - er, Where the sur - ges cease to roll.

Thou Art Gone to the Grave, &c.

Tune —"Scotland," Key of A.

1. Thou art gone to the grave, but we
   will not deplore thee ;
   Though sorrows and darkness encompass the tomb,
   The Saviour has pass'd through its portals before thee,
   And the lamp of his love is thy guide
   through the gloom.

2. Thou art gone to the grave ; we no
   longer behold thee,
   Nor tread the rough path of the world
   by thy side :
   But the wide arms of mercy are spread to
   enfold thee,
   And sinners may hope, since the Sinless
   has died.

3. Thou art gone to the grave ; and, its
   mansions forsaking,
   Perhaps thy tried spirit in doubt linger'd
   long ;
   But the sunshine of heaven beam'd bright
   on thy waking,
   And the song which thou heardst was
   the seraphim's song.

4. Thou art gone to the grave ; but 'twere
   wrong to deplore thee,
   When God was thy ransom, thy guar-
   dian and guide ;
   He gave thee, and took thee, and soon
   will restore thee,
   Where death hath no sting, since the
   Saviour has died.

Flee to your Mountain.

Published in sheet form, Key of D minor.

1. Flee as a bird to your mountain,
   Thou who art weary of sin ;
   Go to the clear-flowing fountain,
   Were you may wash and be clean.
   Fly, for th' avenger is near thee ;
   Call, and the Saviour will hear thee ;
   He on his bosom will bear thee ;
   O thou who art weary of sin.

2. He will protect thee forevea,
   Wipe ev'ry sad-falling tear ;
   He will forsake thee, O never,
   Cherish'd so tenderly there,
   Haste, then, the hours now are flying ;
   Spend not the moments in sighing ;
   Cease from your sorrow and crying ;
   The Saviour will wipe ev'ry tear.

3. Come, then, to Jesus thy Saviour,
   He will redeem thee from sin ;
   Bless with a sense of his favor,
   Make thee all glorious within.
   Call, for thee Saviour is near thee,
   Waiting in mercy to hear thee,
   And by his presence to cheer ehee,
   O thou who art weary of sin.

Asleep in Jesus.

Tune.—"Rest," Oriola 72, Key E flat.

1. Asleep in Jesus ! blessed sleep !
   From which none ever wakes to weep ;
   A calm and undisturb'd repose,
   Unbroken by the last of foes.

2. Asleep in Jesus ! Oh, how sweet
   To be for such a slumber meet !
   With holy confidence to sing
   That Death has lost his cruel sting.

3. Asleep in Jesus ! peaceful rest !
   Whose waking is supremely blest ;
   No fear, no woe, shall dim that hour
   That manifests the Saviour's power.

Sister Thou Wast Mild, &c.

MUSICAL LEAVES 17, Key of C.

1. Sister,* thou wast mild and lovely.
   Gentle as the summer breeze ;
   Pleasant as the air of ev'ning,
   When it floats among the trees.

2. Peaceful be thy silent slumber,
   Peaceful in the grave so low ;
   Thou no more wilt join our number,
   Thou no more our songs shalt know.

3. Dearest sister, thou hast left us,
   Here thy loss we deeply feel ;
   But 'tis God that has bereft us,
   He can still our sorrow heal.

4. Yet again we hope to meet thee,
   When the day of life is fled ;
   Then, in heaven with joy to greet thee,
   Where no farewell tear is shed.

* Brother, or schoolmate.

Thy Will be Done !

SILVER CHIMES 88, Key of E flat.

1. "Thy will be | done ! | In devious way
   The hurrying stream of | life may | run‖
   Yet still our grateful hearts shall say |
   "Thy will be | done."

2. "Thy will be | done !" | If o'er us shine
   A gladdening and a | prosperous | sun‖
   This prayer will make it more divine |
   "Thy will be | done !"

3. "Thy will be | done !" | Though
   shrouded o'er
   Our | path with | gloom, ‖ one comfort,
   one
   Is ours : to breathe, while we adore |
   "Thy will be | done !"
   "Thy will be | done !"

Requiem.

H. R. Palmer.

Slow.

1. Gone. gone, gone from our home, God hath recalled thee In thy youthful bloom,

2. Gone, gone, gone to thy tomb; But 'tis not cheerless, Hope dispels its gloom,

3. Gone, gone, gone to the blest; Earth had its pleasures, But 'twas not thy rest;

rit.   *pp*

Death's i - cy fingers Rest up-on thee now; Still beauty lin-gers On thy pal-lid brow.

While we are weeping O'er the hallow'd ground, Thou art but sleeping 'Till the trump shall sound.

Sin and tempta-tion Were thy sorrow *here*, Then full sal-va - tion Is thy portion *there.*

The Reaper and the Flowers.

From Manual of Music, by permission.   Adapted by W. Ludden.

1.	{ There is a Reaper whose name is Death, and with his .... }	sic-kle keen,	{ He reaps the bearded grain at a breath, And the .... }	flow'rs that grow be-tween.
2	{ "Shall I have naught that is fair?" saith he; "Have naught but the .... }	bearded grain?	{ Tho' the breath of these flow'rs is sweet to me, I'll give ...... }	them all back a-gain."
3	{ He gazed at the flow'rs with tearful eyes, He kiss-d their.. }	drooping leaves;	{ It was for the Lord in Paradise, He.... }	bound them in his [sheaves.
4.	{ "My Lord has need of these flow'rets gay," The Reaper... }	said and smil'd	{ "Dear tokens of the earth are they, Where }	He was once a child."
5.	{ "They shall all bloom in fields of light, Transplanted....... }	by my care,	{ And saints upon their garments white These }	sacred blossoms wear.
6.	{ And the mother gave in tears and pain, The flowers she.... }	most did love;	{ She knew she should find them all again In the................. }	fields of light above.
7.	{ O, not in cruelty, not in wrath, The Reaper.......... }	came that day;	{ 'Twas an angel visit-ed the green earth, And .... }	took the flow'rs away.

With Banner and Badge, &c.

Tune.—"Auld Lang Syne," Key of F.

1. With banner and with badge we come,
   An army true and strong,
To fight against the hosts of rum,
   And this shall be our song.
   CHORUS.
We love the clear cold-water springs,
   Supplied by gentle showers,
We feel the strength cold water brings
   The victory is ours.

2. "Cold-Water Army" is our name :
   Oh, may we faithful be,
And so in truth and justice claim
   The blessings of the free.
      We love the clear, &c.

3. Though others love their rum and wine
   And drink till they are mad,
To water we will still incline,
   To make us strong and glad.
      We love the clear, &c.

4. I pledge to thee this hand of mine,
   In faith and friendship strong ;
And, fellow-soldiers, we will join
   The chorus of our song.
      We love the clear, &c.

O Carry Me Back to My Mother's Home.

SONG QUEEN 22, Key of D.

1. The day was gone, and the night was
      dark,
   And the howling winds went by,
And the blinding sleet fell thick and fast,
   From a stern and stormy sky :
When a mournful wail, through the rush-
      ing gale,
   Was heard at a cottage door—
" O, carry me back, O, carry me back
   To my mother's home once more."
CHO.—Listen to that mournful wailing,
   As it floats to yonder cottage door—
" O, give me back my happy childhood,
   O take me to my home once more."

2. 'Twas a youth who had left his moun-
      tain home :
   He had wandered far and long :
He had drained the goblet's fiery tide,
   At the festal, midnight throng ;
But a dream of home came o'er his heart
   As he crept to the cottage door—
O, carry me back, O, carry me back
   To my mother's home once more."
      CHO.—Listen, &c.

3. "I have left the halls of the tempter's
      power,
   And the revel wild and high ;

They cared not in their reckless mirth
   If I wandered alone to die—
Doth the fire still burn on the household
      hearth,
   By the elm tree old and hoar ?
O, carry me back, O, carry me back
   To my mother's home once more."
      CHO.—Listen, &c.

4. Like the weary bird that hath wander-
      ed long,
   I will seek my mountain nest,
And lay my aching head once more
   On my gentle mother's breast.
Once more will I seek the household
      hearth,
   By the elm tree old and hoar—
O, carry me back, O, carry me back
   To my mother's home once more."
      CHO.—Listen, &c.

In the Ways of True, &c.

Tune.—"Buy a Broom," S. S. Hosanna 156, Key
      of G.

1. In the ways of true temperance see
      children delighting,
   So joyful and happy wherever we go ;
If firm to the purpose in which we're
      uniting,
   We shall never be drunkards—oh, never,
      oh, no !
         Oh, never, oh, no !

2. The pledge we have taken must never
      be broken,
Although the poor drunkard may angrier
      grow ;
We must always remember the words we
      have spoken,
   And never be drunkards,—oh, never,
      oh, no !
         Oh, never, oh, no !

3. The first little drop of strong drink
      that is taken
   Is the first step to ruin, e'en children
      may know ;
If the first little drop be in earnest for-
      saken,
   We shall never be drunkards,—oh,
      never, oh, no !
         Oh, never, oh, no !

4. Then, free from the ruin strong drink
      would occasion,
   We'll stand by our temperance wher-
      ever we go ;
And if bad men should tempt, we'll resist
      their persuasion,
   And never be drunkards,—oh, never,
      oh, no !
         Oh, never, oh, no !

Rev. R. Lowry, by permission.

1. When life's la - bor - song is sung, And the e - bon arch is sprung,
2. Dark the shadows in the vale, Fierce the howl-ing of the gale,
3. Flood the heart with parting tears, Frost the head with pass-ing years,

O'er the shaded couch of death so still; Then the Lord will light the scene,
But the shining ones are near our door; With our robes as bright as they
Min - gle want and woe to - geth - er here; But the Lord will lift the cloud,

With the an - gels' star - ry sheen, As they welcome us to Zi - on's hill.
We will tread the star - ry way, With the sha - dow and the storm no more
That en-wraps the shin - ing crowd, And we'll nev-er know a sor - row there.

Refrain.
Steady time.

We'll meet each oth - er there, Yes, we'll meet each oth - er there, With the

an - gels in the air, Yes, we'll meet each oth-er there; We'll meet each other there,

Yes, we'll meet each oth-er there, With the an-gels, with the an - gels in the air.

Friends of Freedom!

Tune.—" Bruce's, Address," S. S. Hosanna 157,
       Key of A.

1. Friends of freedom ! swell the song,
Young and old, the strain prolong,
Make the temperance army strong,
    And on to victory !
Lift your banners, let them wave,
Onward march, a world to save :
Who would fill a drunkard's grave
    And bear his infamy ?

2. Shrink not when the foe appears ;
Spurn the coward's guilty fears ;
Hear the shrieks, behold the tears,
    Of ruin'd families !
Raise the cry in every spot,
" *Touch not, taste not, handle not !*"
Who would be a drunken sot,
    The worst of miseries ?

3. Give the aching bosom rest :
Carry joy to every breast ;
Make the wretched drunkard blest,
    By living soberly :
Raise the glorious watchword high,
" *Touch not, taste not, till you die !*
Let the echo reach the sky,
    And earth keep jubilee.

4. God of mercy, hear us plead :
For thy help we intercede :
See how many bosoms bleed,
    And heal them speedily.
Haste, oh, haste the happy day
When beneath its gentle ray,
TEMPERANCE all the world shall sway,
    And reign triumphantly.

Softly the Drunkard's Wife, &c.

Tune.—"Gaily the Troubadour," S. S. Hosanna
       157, Key of F.

1. Softly the drunkard's wife breatheth
    her prayer ;
Sadly her bosom heaves, wild with des-
    pair ;
Saying, For thee I pine, mourning alone :
Wanderer, wanderer, come to thy home.

2. He with the revellers merrily sung,
Wildly he raised his voice, madly in song ;
She in a murmuring voice blended her
    tone,
Wanderer, wanderer, come to thy home.

3. Hark ! 'tis her husband's voice rings in
    her ear,
See how her upturn'd eye melts with the
    tear :
Wife of my bosom ! see, I am come !
Come, like a wanderer, back to my home.

4. Brightly the drunkard's home shines in
    the ray,

Sweetly the drunkard's wife smileth to·
    day ;
Drunkard no longer, her husband is come :
Happiness, happiness, brightens their
    home !

Sparkling and Bright.

S. S. HOSANNA 156, Key of B flat.

1. Sparkling and bright in its liquid light
Is the water in our glasses :
'Twill give you health, 'twill give you
    wealth,
Ye lads and rosy lasses !
       CHORUS.
Oh, then, resign your ruby wine,
    Each smiling son and daughter
There's nothing so good for the youthful
    blood,
    Or sweet as the sparkling water.

2. Better than gold is the water cold,
    From the crystal fountain flowing,
A calm delight, both day and night,
    To happy homes bestowing.
       Oh, then, resign, &c.

3. Sorrow has fled from the heart that
    bled,
    Of the weeping wife and mother :
They've given up the poison-cup,
    Son, husband, daughter, brother.
       Oh, then, resign, &c.

Go, Go, Thou that Enslavest me.

S. S. HOSANNA 157, Key of G.

1. Go, go, thou that enslavest me,
    Now, now, thy power is o'er,
Long, long, have I obey'd thee ;
    Now I'll not drink any more.
       No, no, no, no !
    No, I'll not drink any more.

2. Thou, thou, bringest me ever,
    Deep, deep sorrow and pain !
Then, then, from thee I'll sever,
    Now I'll not serve then again.
       No, no, no, no !
    No, I'll not serve thee again.

3. Rum, rum, thou hast bereft me,
    Home, friends, pleasure so sweet ;
Now, now, forever I've left thee,
    Thou and I never shall meet.
       No, no, no, no !
    Thou and I never shall meet.

4. Joys, joys bright as the morning,
    Now, now, on me will pour ;
Hope, hope, sweetly is dawning,
    Now I'll not drink any more.
       No, no, no, no !
    No, I'll not drink any more.

To be sung at the grave.　　　　　H. R. PALMER. (1862.)

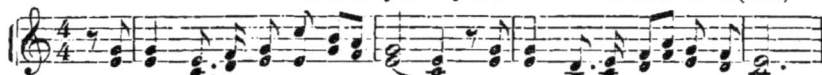

1. She sleeps in the val-ley so sweet,　A - bove her the green willows wave;
2. How calm-ly she rest-ed in God;　"To thy arms, my Sa - vior, I come;

We planted the rose at her feet,　To bloom and de-cay o'er her grave.
Come quickly, come quickly, O Lord,　And welcome thy wan-der - er home!"

She sleeps in the val - ley so sweet,　No sound e'er dis-turbs her re - pose;
She sleeps in the val - ley so sweet,　Her spir - it has tak - en its flight;

So qui - et in this calm re- treat,　She rests safe, secure from life's woes.
Her form is but dust 'neath our feet,　While she is an an - gel of light.

Refrain.

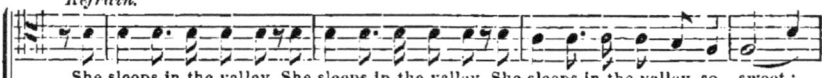

She sleeps in the valley, She sleeps in the valley, She sleeps in the valley so sweet;

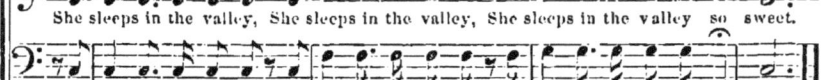

She sleeps in the valley, She sleeps in the valley, She sleeps in the valley so sweet;

She sleeps in the valley, She sleeps in the valley, She sleeps in the valley so sweet;

pp

She sleeps in the valley, She sleeps in the valley, She sleeps in the valley so sweet.

She sleeps in the valley, She sleeps in the valley, She sleeps in the valley so sweet.

pp

She sleeps in the valley, She sleeps in the valley, She sleeps in the valley so sweet.

Published in sheet form with piano accompaniment by J. L. PETERS, New York.

On a Christmas Morning.

G. SHOWER, 6, Key of D; also Oriola 82, S. S.
Hosanna 106.

1. Little children, can you tell,
Do you know the story well,
Every girl and every boy,
Why the angels sing for joy
‖: On the Christmas morning :‖
The angels sing for joy?

2. Shepherds sat upon the ground,
Fleecy flocks were scatter'd round,
When the brightness fill'd the sky,
And a song was heard on high,
CHO.—On the Christmas morning.

3. " Joy and peace," the angels sang,
Far the pleasant echoes rang,
" Peace on earth, to men good will !"
Hark! the angels sing it still
CHO.—On the Christmas morning.

4. For a little babe that day,
Christ, the Lord of angels lay,
Born on earth our Lord to be:
This the wondering angels see,
CHO.—On the Christmas morning.

5. Let us sing the angels' song,
And the pleasant sounds prolong:
This fair Babe of Bethlehem
Children loves and blesses them
CHO.—On the Christmas morning.

6. " Peace" our little hearts shall fill,
" Peace on earth, to men good will !"
Hear us sing the angels' song,
And the pleasant notes prolong,
CHO.—On the Christmas morning.

Christmas Carol.

Tune.—" WALK IN THE LIGHT," S. S. BELL, No.
1—60, Key of G; also G. Chain 43,

1. Loudly let the anthem swell,
On this night, on this night,
Joyously the story tell,
On this Christmas night;
For the Saviour's wondrous birth,
God we praise, God we praise,
Peace He brought to all on earth,
Thee, Oh God, we praise!
CHORUS.—Let us swell the glad song,
Swell the song, swell the song,
Let us swell the glad song,
On this Christmas night.

2. Shepherds, watching on the plain,
On this night, on this night,
Heard the angels' heavenly strain,
On this Christmas night;
Bright the glory shone around,

In the night, in the night,
Hasting, then, the babe they found,
Ere the morning light.
CHO.—Let us swell the, &c.

3. In a manger, Jesus lay,
On this night, on this night,
While above, His star did stay,
On this Christmas night;
Then the shepherds quick returned,
Praising God, praising God,
Telling all the news they'd learned,
On this Christmas night.
CHO.—Let us swell the, &c.

4. Age on age has passed, yet we,
On this night, on this night,
Gather round our Christmas tree,
On this Christmas night;
Here we praise the Saviour's name,
On this night, on this night,
Joyous sing the angels' strain,
On this Christmas night.
CHO.—Let us swell the, &c.
Dr. C. R. Blackall.

The Song of Angels.

G. CHAIN 114, Key of G; also S. S. Hosanna, 88.

1. There's a song the angels sing,
And its notes with rapture ring,
Round the throne whose radiance fills the
heavens above.
Shepherds heard the distant strain,
Watching on Judea's plain,
" Glory be to God, to men be peace and
love !"
CHORUS.
Through the earth and through the
sky
Let the anthem ever fly,
" Peace, good will to men, and glory be to
God on high !"

2. 'Tis a song for children too;
To the Saviour 'tis their due;
Let its grateful notes ascend to him again;
Join with angels in their song,
And the heavenly strain prolong,
" Glory be to God, good will and peace to
men !"
CHO.—Through the earth, &c

3. Soon around that throne may we
With those happy angels be,
Striking harps to strains that nevermore
shall cease:
Mingling love with loftiest praise,
Still the chorus there we'll raise,
" Glory be to God, to men good will and
peace !"
CHO.—Through the earth, &c.

1. Our Christmas Tree is deck'd once more, In joy we meet a-round;
2. Our Christmas Tree is fresh and green, While skies are cold and drear;
8. Our Christmas Tree is shin-ing bright, While eve-ning shades surround;
4. Kind friends! whose hands have deck'd this tree, Our grate-ful thanks re-cieve;

It tells of bright-er things in store, Let songs of praise re-sound.
Its har-vest store of fruit is seen, When win-ter blights the year.
Thus God doth give His chil-dren light When dark-ness falls a-round.
Yet, Lord! for Christmas joys, to Thee Our high-est praise we give.

Refrain.

The Christmas Tree a-gain, So beau-ti-ful and bright,

The Christmas Tree a-gain, So beau-ti-ful and bright,

The Christmas Tree a-gain, It blooms for us to-night.

The Christmas Tree a-gain, It blooms for us to-night.

My Country 'Tis of Thee.

G. CHAIN 103, Key of G ; also S. S. Hosanna 94,
P. Songs 125.

1. My country, 'tis of thee,
Sweet land of liberty,
  Of thee I sing ;
Land where my fathers died ;
Land of the pilgrims' pride ;
From every mountain-side
  Let freedom ring.

2. My native country, thee,
Land of the noble free,
  Thy name I love ;
I love thy rocks and rills,
Thy woods and templed hills ;
My heart with rapture thrills
  Like that above.

3. Let music swell the breeze,
And ring from all the trees
  Sweet freedom's song ;
Let mortal tongues awake ;
Let all that breathe partake ;
Let rocks their silence break,
  The sound prolong.

O Say Can You See.

Key of B flat.

1. O say can you see, by the dawns early
  light,
What so proudly we hailed at the twilight's
  last gleaming ?
Whose broad stripes and bright stars thro'
  the perilous fight,
O'er the ramparts we watch'd, were so
  gallantly streaming ;
And the rocket's red glare, the bombs
  bursting in air,
Gave proof thro' the night that our flag
  was still there ;
O say, does the star spangled banner still
  wave,
O'er the land of the free, and the home of
  the brave ?

2. On the shore, dimly seen through the
  mist of the deep,
Where the foe's haughty host in dread
  silence reposes,
What is that, which the breeze o'er the
  towering steep,
As it fitfully blows, half conceals, half dis-
  closes ?
Now it catches the gleam of the morning's first beam,
In full glory reflected now shines on the
  stream ;
'Tis the star-spangled banner, oh, long
  may it wave
O'er the land of the free, and the home of
  the brave.

3. Oh, thus be it ever, when freemen shall
  stand

Between their loved home and war's desolation ;
Bless'd with victory and peace, may the
  heaven-rescued land
Praise the power that hath made and preserved us a nation.
Then conquer we must, when our cause
  it is just,
And this be our motto—" In God is our
  trust !"
And the star-spangled banner in triumph
  shall wave
O'er the land of the free and the home of
  the brave.

Hail ! Our Country's Natal Morn.

SONG QUEEN, Key of B flat.

1. Hail our country's natal morn !
Hail our spreading kindred born !
Hail thou banner not yet torn !
  Still waving o'er the FREE !
While this day, in festal throng,
Millions swell the patriot song,
Shall not we thy notes prolong?
  Hallowed Jubilee !

CHO.—Hail ! our country's natal morn,
  Hail ! ye millions yet unborn,
  Hail ! thou banner not yet torn,
    Still waving o'er the free.
  While this day, in festal throng,
  Millions swell the patriot song,
  Shall not we thy notes prolong,
    Hallowed jubilee ?

2. Who would sever Freedom's shrine?
Who would draw th' invidious line ?
Though by birth one spot be mine,
  Yet dear is all the rest—
Dear to me the SOUTH's fair land,
Dear the central mountain band,
Dear NEW ENGLAND's rocky strand,
  Dear the prairied WEST.
    CHO.—Hail ! our country's, &c.

3. By our altars pure and free,
By our law's deep-rooted tree,
By the past dread memory,
  And by our MARTYR's name :
By our common parent tongue,
By our hopes, bright, buoyant, young,
By the tie of country strong,
  United we'll remain.
    CHO.—Hail ! our country's, &c.

4. Brothers ! have ye bled in vain ?
Ages ! must ye droop again ?
Maker ! shall we rashly stain
  These blessings sent by THEE ?
No ! receive our solemn vow,
While before thy throne we bow,
Ever to maintain as now,
  " UNION—LIBERTY."
    CHO.—Hail ! our country's, &c.

With Christ we'll Walk the Wayside.

"Dear little children; I want you all to be ready to die; ready that you may go to be with Christ, WITH CHRIST, WITH CHRIST.'

FREDERICK STARR, JR. [Dying message to his Sunday School.]

Words by Rev. H. C. M'COOK   Music by JAS. M. NORTH. By permission.

1. The feet for - sake the beat - en path, And far in er - ror stray:
2. The heart, be-guiled by Sa-tan's voice, With long - ing fol-lows sin:
3. Dark is the path, when sorrow broods Black wing'd up - on the way;

4. Swift runs the day of life a - long, The twi - light hour is nigh:
5. They soft-ly rest who sleep with Christ, With shout-ings shall they rise,
6. Sweet is the world, and sweet is life, And sweet with friends to stay;

But true and right will be their walk, With Christ to guide the way.
But turns and cleaves to Ho - li - ness, With Christ to dwell with - in.
With Christ bright Morn-ing Star a - bove, The dark-ness shines as day.

With Christ to gild the ev'ning clouds, Bright glows the sun - set sky.
And mount to reign e - ter - nal years, With Christ in Par - a - dise.—
But sweet - er, bet - ter to de - part, And be with Christ for aye.

Refrain.

With Christ we'll walk the way - side, With Christ de - scend the vale;

With Christ a - rise, and mount the skies, With Christ for - ev - er dwell.

Come, Thou Almighty King, &c.

Tune.—America, Key of G.

1. Come, thou Almighty King,
Help us thy name to sing,
  Help us to praise !
Father all-glorious,
O'er all victorious,
Come and reign over us,
  Ancient of days.

2. Jesus, our Lord, arise,
Scatter our enemies,
  Now make them fall !
Let thine almighty aid
Our sure defence be made,
Our souls on thee be stay'd :
  Lord, hear our call !

3. Come, thou incarnate Word,
Gird on thy mighty sword ;
  Our prayer attend !
Come, and thy people bless ;
Come, give thy word success :
Spirit of holiness,
  On us descend !

Columbia, the Gem of, &c.

Key of G.

1. O, Columbia ! the gem of the ocean,
  The home of the brave and the free,
The shrine of each patriot's devotion,
  A world offers homage to thee !
Thy mandates make heroes assemble,
  When Liberty's form stands in view,—
Thy banners make tyranny tremble,
  When borne by the Red, White, and
    Blue.
Cho.—‖:When borne by the Red, White,
    and Blue,:‖
Thy banners make tyranny tremble,
When borne by the Red, White, and Blue.

2. When war winged its wide desolation,
  And threatened the land to deform,
The ark, then, of Freedom's foundation,
  Columbia, rode safe through the storm ;
With her garlands of vict'ry around her,
  When so proudly she bore her brave
    crew,
With her flag proudly floating before her,
  The boast of the Red, White, and Blue.
Cho.—The boast of the Red, &c.

3. The wine-cup,the wine-cup bring hither,
  And fill you it true to the brim !
May the wreaths they have won never
    wither,
  Nor the stars of their glory grow dim !
May the service united ne'er sever,
  But they to their colors prove true !
The Army and Navy forever !
  Three cheers for the Red, White, and
    Blue !

The Marseillaise.

Key of G.

1. Ye sons of Freedom wake to glory,
  Hark ! hark, what myriads bid you rise,
Your children,wives, and grandsires hoary
  ‖:Behold their tears, and hear their
    cries !:‖
Shall lawless tyrants mischief breeding,
  With hireling host, a ruffian band
Affright and desolate the land,
While peace and liberty lie bleeding.
Cho.—To arms, to arms, ye brave,
  The patriot sword unsheath,
March on, march on, all hearts resolved
  On liberty or death.

2. Oh, liberty ! can man resign thee,
  Once having felt thy glorious flame ?
Can tyrant's bolts and bars confine thee,
  ‖:And thus thy noble spirit tame ?:‖
Too long our country wept bewailing
  The bloodstain'd sword our conquerors
    wield,
But freedom is our sword and shield,
And all their arts, are unavailing.
  Cho.—To arms, &c.

Star of Bethlehem.

Mason's Book of Chants 133, Key of A.

1. When marshall'd on the nightly plain,
  The glittering host be- | stud the | sky,
One star alone, of all the train,
  Can fix the | sinner's | wandering | eye.‖
Hark ! hark ! to God the chorus breaks,
  From every host, from | ev'ry | gem ;
But one alone the Saviour speaks,—
  It is the | Star, the | Star of | Beth-
    lehem !

2. Once on the raging seas I rode ;
  The storm was loud, the | night was |
    dark,
The ocean yawn'd, and rudely blow'd
  The wind that | toss'd my | foundering
    | bark‖
Deep horror then my vitals froze,
  Death-struck, I ceas'd the | tide to—
    stem ;
When suddenly a star arose,—
  It was the | Star, the | Star of | Bethle-
    hem !

3. It was my guide, my light, my all :
  It made my dark fore- | bodings | cease;
And through the storm, and danger's
    thrall,
  It | led me to the | port of | peace.‖
Now safely moor'd, my perils o'er,
  I'll sing, | first in | night's | diadem,
For ever and for evermore,
  The | Star ! the | Star of | Bethlehem !
    H. K. White.

Cast thy Bread upon the Waters.

By H. R. PALMER.

1. Cast thy bread up-on the wa-ters, Ye who have but scant sup-ply,
2. Cast thy bread up-on the wa-ters, Poor and wea-ry worn with care,
8. Cast thy bread up-on the wa-ters, You who have a-bund-ant store,
4. Cast thy bread up-on the wa-ters, Far and wide your treasures strew,
5. Cast thy bread up-on the wa-ters, Waft it on with praying breath,

An-gel eyes will watch a-bove it You shall find it by-and-bye
Of-ten sit-ting in the shad-ow, Have you not a crumb to spare?
It may float on ma-ny bil-lows, It may strand on many a shore,
Scat-ter it with will-ing fin-gers, Laugh for joy to see it go!
In some dis-tant doubtful mo-ment, It may save a soul from death.

He who in his right-eous bal-ance Doth each hu-man ac-tion weigh,
Can you not to those a-round you, Sing some lit-tle song of hope,
You may think it lost for-ev-er, But as sure as God is true,
For if you too close-ly keep it, It will on-ly drag you down;
When you sleep in sol-emn si-lence, 'Neath the morn and even-ing dew,

Will your sac-ri-fice re-mem-ber, Will your lov-ing deed re-pay,
As you look, with long-ing vis-ion, Through Faith's mighty tele-scope,
In this life, or in the oth-er It will yet re-turn to you,
If you love it more than Je-sus It will keep you from your crown,
Stranger hands which you have strengthened May strew lillies o-ver you

The Rainy Day.

Published in sheet form, Key of F.

1. The day is cold, and dark, and dreary;
It rains, and the wind is never weary;
The vine still clings to the mouldering
wall,
But at every gust the dead leaves fall
‖:And the day is dark and dreary.:‖

2. My life is cold, and dark, and dreary:
It rains, and the wind is never weary;
My thoughts still cling to the mouldering
past,
But the hopes of youth fall thick in the
blast,
‖:And the days are dark and dreary.:‖

3. Be still, sad heart ! and cease repining;
Behind the clouds is the sun still shining;
Thy fate is the common fate of all,
Into each life some rain must fall,
‖:Some days must be dark and dreary.:‖
Longfellow.

The River of Time.

Published in sheet form, Key of F.

1. There's a magical isle up the river of
Time,
Where the softest of airs are playing;
There's a cloudless sky and a tropical
clime,
And a song as sweet as a vesper chime,
And the tunes with the roses are stray-
ing.

2. And the name of this isle is the Long
Ago,
And we bury our treasures there.
There are brows of beauty and bosoms of
snow—
There are heaps of dust, but we love them
so !
There are trinkets and tresses of hair.

3. There are fragments of song that no-
body sings,
And a part of an infant's prayer ;
There's a lute unswept and a harp with-
out strings,
There are broken vows and pieces of rings,
And the garments that *she* used to wear.

4. There are hands that are waved when
the fairy shore,
By the mirage, is lifted in air ;
And we sometimes hear, through the tur-
bulant roar,
Sweet voices we heard in the days gone
before,
When the wind down the river is fair.
B. F. Taylor.

Sunday School Volunteer Song.

FRESH LAURELS 30, Key of A.

1. We are marching on, with shield and
banner bright,
We will work for God and battle for the
right ;
We will praise his name, rejoicing in his
might,
And we'll work till Jesus calls :
In the Sunday School our army we pre-
pare,
As we rally round our blessed standard
there ;
And the Saviour's cross we early learn to
bear,
While we work till Jesus calls.
CHO.—Then awake, then awake,
Happy song, happy song,
Shout for joy, shout for joy,
As we gladly march along :
We are marching onward, singing as we go,
To the promised land, where living waters
flow ;
Come and join our ranks as pilgrims here
below,
Come and work till Jesus calls.

2. We are marching on, our Captain ever
near,
Will protect us still, his voice we ever
hear ;
Let the foe advance, we'll never, never
fear,
For we'll work till Jesus calls.
Then awake, awake, our happy, happy
song,
We will shout for joy, and gladly march
along ;
In the Lord of Hosts let every heart be
strong,
While we work till Jesus calls.
CHO.—Then awake, &c.

3. We are marching on the straight and
narrow way,
That will lead to life and everlasting day,
To the smiling fields that never will decay,
But we'll work till Jesus calls :
We are marching on, and pressing toward
the prize,
To a glorious crown beyond the glowing
skies,
To the radiant fields where pleasure never
dies,
And we'll work till Jesus calls.
CHO.—Then awake, &c.

Doxology.

Praise God from whom all blessing flow,
Praise him all creatures here below ;
Praise him above ye heavenly host,
Praise Father, Son, and Holy Ghost.

Tried and True.

Words by FANNY CROSBY.

W. H. DOANE.

1. We are a band of mer-ry chil-dren, Full of glee, full of glee,
2. "Hap-py am I," the bird is sing-ing, Wild and free, wild and free,
3. "Hap-py am I," the wind is sigh-ing, Thro' the shade, thro' the shade;

Like the spring-time in its beau-ty, Glad are we, glad are we.
While to the song with hearts we ech-o, So are we, so are we;
"Sweet is my home" the dai-sy mur-murs, In the glade, in the glade,

Bright is the bu-sy world a-round us, Bright with flow'rs, Bright with flow'rs,
O! there is joy in ev'-ry blos-som, We may share, We may share,
Thus we can say in days of child-hood, Full of glee, Full of glee,

Smiles from the sun-ny vale a-bove us, Come with the hours, Come with the hours.
While we a-dore the hand that made it, Pure and fair, Pure and fair.
Blending our hearts with na-ture's voi-ces, Blest are we, Blest are we.

Refrain.

We are a band of mer-ry, mer-ry children, While to the Sun-day-school we cling,

We are a band of mer-ry, mer-ry chil-dren, Tried and true, tried and true.

If I Were a Voice.

Song Crown 174, Key of A.

1. If I were a voice, a persuasive voice,
    That could travel the wide world thro'
I would fly on the beams of the morning
    light.
And speak to men with a gentle might,
    And tell them to be true.
I would fly, I would fly over land and sea,
Wherever a human heart might be,
Telling a tale or singing a song
In praise of the right—in blame of the
    wrong,
    I would fly, I would fly,
    I would fly o'er land and sea.

2. If I were a voice, a consoling voice,
    I'd fly on the wings of the air :
The homes of sorrow and guilt I'd seek,
And calm and truthful words I'd speak,
    To save them from despair.
I would fly, I would fly o'er the crowded
    town,
And drop, like the happy sunlight, down
Into the hearts of suffering men,
And teach them to look up again,
    I would fly, I would fly,
    I would fly o'er the crowded town.

3. If I were a voice, a convincing voice
    I'd travel with the wind,
And wherever I saw the nations torn,
By warfare, jealousy, spite, or scorn,
    Or hatred of their kind,
I would fly, I would fly on the thunder
    crash,
And into their blinded bosoms flash ;
Then, with their evil thoughts subdued,
I'd teach them Christian Brotherhood,
    I would fly, I would fly,
    I would fly on the thunder crash.

4. If I were a voice, an immortal voice,
    I would fly the earth around :
And wherever man to his idols bowed,
I'd publish in notes both long and loud
    The Gospel's joyful sound.
I would fly, I would fly on the wings of
    day,
Proclaiming peace on my world-wide way,
Bidding the saddened earth rejoice—
If I were a voice, an immortal voice,
    I would fly, I would fly,
    I would fly on the wings of day.

A Hundred Years to Come.

Song Crown 147, Key of A.

1 Where, where will be the birds that sing?
    A hundred years to come ?
The flow'rs that now in beauty spring,
    A hundred years to come ?
The rosy lip, the lofty brow,

The heart that beats so gaily now ?
O where will be love's beaming eye,
Joy's pleasant smile, and sorrow's sigh ?
Chorus.—‖:A hundred years to come ?·‖
    Where ? where ? where ?
    A hundred years to come .

2. Who'll throng for gold this crowded
    street,
    A hundred years to come ?
Who'll tread yon church with willing feet?
    A hundred years to come ?
Pale, trembling age, and fiery youth,
And childhood with its heart of truth ?
The rich, the poor, on land and sea—
Where will the mighty millions be ?
    Cho.—A hundred years to come, &c.

3. We all within our graves shall sleep,
    A hundred years to come ;
No living soul for us will weep,
    A hundred years to come ;
But other men our lands will till,
And others, then, our streets will fill,
While other birds will sing as gay—
As bright the sun shine as to-day,
    Cho.—A hundred years to come, &c.

O, Eyes That are Weary, &c.

Tune.—"Expostulation," Key of G.

1. O, eyes that are weary, and hearts that
    are sore !
Look off unto Jesus, now sorrow no more!
The light of his countenance shineth so
    bright,
That here, as in heaven, there need be no
    night.

2. While looking to Jesus, my heart can
    not fear ;
I tremble no more when I see Jesus near :
I know that his presence my safe-guard
    will be,
For " Why are ye troubled ?" he saith un-
    to me.

3. Still looking to Jesus, oh, may I be
    found,
When Jordan's dark waters encompass
    me round :
They bear me away in his presence to be:
I see him still nearer whom always I see.

4. Then, then shall I know the full beauty
    and grace
Of Jesus, my Lord, when I stand face to
    face ;
Shall know how his love went before me
    each day,
And wonder that ever my eyes turned
    away.

Lead us Home.

Words by F. F. PALGRAVE. Music by SAMUEL WILLARD, M. D.

1. Star of morn and ev - en, Sun of Heav-en's Heav - en,
2. Sav - ior pure and ho - ly, Lov - er of the low - ly,
3. Star of morn and ev - en, Shine on us from Heav - en,

Sav-ior high and dear! Towards us turn thine ear! Thro' whate'er may
Sign us with thy sign: Take our hands in thine; Take our hands and
From thy glo - ry throne: Hear thy ve - ry own: Lord and Sa - vior

come, Thou canst lead us, lead us home, Thou canst lead us home.
come, Lead thy children, lead us home, Lead thy children home.
come; Lead us, lead us to our home, Lead us to our home.

Refrain.

Home! home! home! Lead us dear Sa - vior, with ten - der hand,

Home! home! home! Lead us dear Sa - vior, with ten - der hand,

Repeat p p

Bring us all home, Bring us all home to the heav'n - ly land.

Bring us all home, Bring us all home to the heav'n - ly land.

Morning Prayer.

(For music to the following Chants see Olive
Branch 297 and 298.)

Venite Exultimus Domino.

Key of D.

1. O Come, let us sing un- | to the | Lord ‖
let us heartily rejoice in the | strength of
| our sal- | vation. ‖

2. Let us come before his presence | with
thanks- | giving, ‖ and show ourselves |
glad in | him with | psalms.

3. For the Lord is a | great= | God ‖ and
a great | King a | bove all | gods.

4. In his hand are all the corners | of the
| earth ; ‖ and the strength of the | hills
is | his= | also.

5. The sea is his, | and he | made it ; ‖ and
his hands pre- | pared the | dry= | land.

6. O come, let us worship | and | fall |
down, ‖ and kneel be- | fore the | Lord
our | Maker.

7. For he is the | Lord our | God, ‖ and
we are people of his pasture, and the |
sheep of | his= | hand.

8. O worship the Lord in the | beauty of
| holiness ; ‖ let the whole earth | stand
in | awe of | him.

9. For he cometh, for he cometh to | judge
the | earth ‖ and with righteousness to
judge the world, and the | people | with
his | truth.

10. Glory be to the Father, and | to the |
Son ‖ and | to the | Holy | Ghost ;

11. As it was in the beginning, is now,
and | ever shall | be ‖ world with- | out
end. | A= | men.

Gloria in Excelsis.

Key of G,

TO THE FIRST PART OF THE CHANT.

1. Glory be to | God on | high, ‖ and on
earth | peace, good | will towards | men.

2. We praise thee, we bless thee, we |
worship | thee, ‖ we glorify thee, we give
thanks to | thee for | thy great | glory.

TO THE SECOND PART.

3. O Lord God, Heavenly King, ‖ God,
the Father Al= | mighty !

4. O Lord, the only-begotten Son, Jesus
| Christ, ‖ O Lord God, Lamb of God,
Son of the | Father.

TO THE THIRD PART.

5. That takest away the | sins of the | world ‖
have mercy up- on= us.

6. Thou that takest away the sins of the
| world, ‖ have mercy up- | on= | us.

7. Thou that takest away the | sins of the
| world, ‖ re- | ceive our | prayer.

8. Thou that sittest at the right hand of
God the Father, ‖ have mercy up- | on=
| us.

TO THE FIRST PART.

9. For thou only | art= | holy, ‖ Thou | on-
ly | art the | Lord.

10. Thou only, O Christ, with the Holy |
Ghost, ‖ art most high in the glory of |
God the | Father. ‖ A- | men.

Te Deum Laudamus.

Tune.—" Rose of Sharon," Key of A flat. Published by Moore, Kelly & Co., Chicago.

1. SOLO.—We praise Thee, O God ; we ac-
knowledge Thee to be the | Lord ; ‖
CHO.—All the earth doth worship Thee,
the Father Ever- | lasting. ‖
SOL.—To Thee, all Angels cry aloud : the
Heavens and all the powers there- | in ; ‖
CHO.—To Thee, Cherubim and Seraphim
con- | tinually do cry. ‖

CHORUS.

2. Holy,—Holy,—Ho- | ly ; ‖
Lord God of | Sabaoth ; ‖
Heaven and earth are | full ; ‖
Of the | majesty of Thy Glory. ‖

3. SOL.—The glorious company of the
Apostles praise | Thee ; ‖
CHO.—The goodly fellowship of the
Prophets praise | Thee ; ‖
SOL.—The noble army of Martyrs praise
| Thee ; ‖
CHO.—The Holy Church, throughout all
the world | doth acknowledge Thee. ‖

4. SOL.—The Father, of an infinite | Maj-
esty ; ‖
CHO.—Thine adorable, true, and only |
Son ; ‖
SOL.—Also the Holy Ghost, the | Com-
forter ; ‖
CHO.—Thou art the King of Glory, O
Christ ; Thou art the Everlasting | Son
—of the Father. ‖

5. SOL.—When Thou tookest upon Thee
to deliver | man ; ‖
CHO.—Thou didst humble Thyself to be
born of a | Virgin ; ‖
SOL.—When Thou hadst overcome the
sharpness of | death ; ‖
CHO—Thou didst open the Kingdom or
| Heaven to all believers. ‖

6. SOL.—Thou sittest on the right hand
of God, in the Glory of the | Father ; ‖
CHO.—We believe that Thou shalt come,
to be our | Judge ; ‖
SOL.—We therefore pray Thee, help Thy
servants, whom Thou hast redeemed
with Thy precious | blood ;

CHO.—Make them to be numbered with thy Saints, in | glory everlasting. ‖

7. SOL.—O Lord, save Thy people, and bless Thine | heritage ; ‖
CHO.—Govern them and lift them up for- | ever. ‖
SOL.—Day by day we magnify | Thee ; ‖
CHO.—And we worship Thy Name ever, | world without—end. ‖

8. SOL.—Vouchsafe, O Lord, to keep us this day without | sin ; ‖
CHO.—O Lord, have mercy upon us, have mercy upon | us. ‖
SOL.—O Lord, let Thy mercy be upon us, as our trust is in | Thee ; ‖
CHO.—O Lord, in Thee have I trusted ; let me | never be confounded. ‖

(For Jubilate Deo, see page 37.)

Benedictus.
Key of F.

1. Blessed be the Lord | God of | Israel, ‖ for he hath visited, | and re- | deemed his | people ;

2. And hath raised up a mighty sal- | vation | for us ‖ in the | house of his | servant | David ;

3. As he spake by the mouth of ⸴his | holy | Prophets, ‖ which have been | since the | world be- | gan ;

4. That we should be saved | from our | enemies ‖ and from the | hand of | all that | hate us.

5. Glory be to the Father, | and to the | Son, ‖ and | to the | Holy | Ghost ;

6. As it was in the beginning, is now, and | ever | shall be, ‖ world with- | out end. A- | men.

(For responses to the Decalogue, see page 84.)

Evening Prayer.
(For Doxology and Gloria in Excelsis, see Morning Prayer.)

Cantate Domino.
Key of G.

1. O sing unto the | Lord a 'new | song ; ‖ for he | hath done | marvellous | things.

2. With his own right hand, and with his | holy | arm, ‖ hath he | gotten him- | self the | victory.

3. The Lord declared | his sal- | vation ; ‖ his righteousness hath he openly showed | in the | sight of the | heathen.

4. He hath remembered his mercy and truth toward the | house of | Israel ; ‖ and

all the ends of the world have seen the sal- | vation | of our | God.

5. Show yourselves joyful unto the Lord, | all ye | lands, ‖ sing, re- | joice, and | give= | thanks.

6. Praise the Lord up- | on the | harp ; | sing to the harp with a | Psalm of | thanks- = | giving.

7. With trumpets, | also, and | shawms, ‖ O show yourself joyful be- | fore the | Lord, the | King.

8. Let the sea make a noise, and all that | therein | is ; ‖ the round world, and | they that | dwell there- | in.

9. Let the floods clap their hands, and let the hills be joyful together be- | fore the | Lord ; ‖ for he | cometh to | judge the | earth.

10. With righteousness shall he | judge the | world, ‖ and the | people | with= | equity.

11. Glory be to the Father, | and to the | Son, ‖ and | to the | Holy | Ghost.

12. As it was in the beginning, is now, an- | ever | shall be, ‖ world with | out end A= | men.

Deus Misereatur.
Key of E flat.

1. God be merciful unto | us, and | bless us, ‖ and show us the light of his countenance, and be | merci- | ful un- | to us.

2. That thy way may be | known upon | earth, ‖ thy saving | health a- | mong all nations.

3. Let the people praise | thee, O | God ‖ yea, let | all the | people | praise thee.

4. O let the nations rejoice | and be | glad, ‖ for thou shalt judge the folk righteously, and govern the | nations | upon | earth.

5. Let the people praise | thee, O | God ‖ yea, let | all the | people | praise thee.

6. Then shall the earth bring | forth her | increase ‖ and God, even our own | God shall | give us his | blessing.

7. God= shall | bless us, ‖ and all the ends of the | world shall | fear= | him.

8. Glory be to the Father, | and to the | Son, ‖ and | to the | Holy | Ghost ;

9. As it was in the beginning, is now, and | ever | shall be, ‖ world with- | out end. A-= | men.

Right Away.

Words by C.

From Bradbury's Fresh Laurels, by permission.

Wm. B. Bradbury.

1. I will come to Je - sus right a - way, right a - way,
2. I will pray to Je - sus right a - way, right a - way,

3. I will live for Je - sus right a - way, right a - way,
4. I will work for Je - sus right a - way, right a - way,

'Tis his Spir - it calls me, I o - bey; Je - sus will re - ceive me,
I will seek his bless - ing ev - ery day; While my heart is plead - ing.

'Tis my Sa - viour calls me, I o - bey; Now in childhood's morning,
La - bor in his vine - yard ev - ery day, With my heart pur - su - ing

He will nev - er leave me, I will come to Je - sus right a -
He is in - ter - ced - ing, I will pray to Je - sus right a -

Is the gen - tle warn - ing, I will live for Je - sus right a -
What my hands are do - ing, I will work for Je - sus ev - ery

way, right a - way, I will come to Je - sus right a - way.
way, right a - way, I will pray to Je - sus right a - way.

way, right a - way, I will live for Je - sus right a - way.
day ev - ery day, I will work for Je - sus ev - ery day.

Jerusalem the Golden.

"Here have we no continuing city, but we seek one to come."

1. Je - ru - sa - lem the gold - en! With milk and ho - ney blest;
2. They stand, those halls of Si - on, All ju - bi - lant with song,
3. There is the throne of Da - vid, And there, from care re - leas'd,
4. O sweet and bless - ed coun - try, The home of God's e - lect,

Be - neath thy con - tem - pla - tion Sink heart and voice op - prest.
And bright with ma - ny an an - gel, And all the mar - tyr throng.

The shout of them that tri - umph, The song of them that feast.
O sweet and bless - ed coun - try, That ea - ger hearts ex - pect!

I know not, oh! I know not What joys a - wait us there;
The prince is ev - er in them, The day - light is se - rene,

And they who with their Lea - der Have con - quer'd in the fight,
Je - sus, in mer - cy bring us To that dear land of rest;

What ra - dian - cy of glo - ry, What bliss be - yond com - pare.
The pas - tures of the bless - ed Are decked in glo - rious sheen.

For - ev - er and for - ev - er Are clad in robes of white.
Who art, with God the Fath - er, And Spir - it ev - er blest. A - men.

Clinging to the Rock.

Composed expressly for the " NORTH STAR MISSION " Sabbath-school, by W. H. DOANE.

Allegro.

1. When the tempest rages high, Sailing on life's boisterous sea; Stormy billows I de-

2. When 'mid drifting wrecks I 'm cast, Darkness settling thickly round, Hope shall lift her
   [light at
3. When the conquering waves shall close Proudly o'er me as I die; Over these brief victor

Chorus.

fy   If I then may on - ly   be   Clinging to the Rock, Clinging to the Rock.

last, If I then be on - ly   found Clinging to the Rock, Clinging to the Rock.
foes, I shal triumph while I   cry, Clinging to the Rock, Clinging to the Rock.

Shel-ter for me ev-er, Strength that faileth never; When the storms of life are o'er,

Shel-ter for me ev-er, Strength that faileth never; When the storms of life are o'er,

Look for me on Canaan's shore,   Clinging to the Rock, Clinging to the Rock.

Look for me on Canaan's   shore,   Clinging to the Rock, Clinging to the Rock.

Words by DR. BLACKALL.　　　　　　　　　Music by GEO. C. PEARSON.

ALLEGRO.

1. Hail! Thou glo - rious name! Wide the news pro-claim! Je-sus, low-ly,
2. Here, this hap - py day, We, our joy - ous lay, Sweetly singing,

Pure and ho-ly, Came, a King from Heaven's high throne; Life he gave us, Died to save us,
Clearly ringing, Lift the songs of praise to Heaven: Je-sus loves us, Smiles, and proves us

CHORUS.

Rose to make us all His own! We sing Ho - sannas to our King, And glad our happy

For last verse.

By the grace which He hath given! Then sweet Hosannas to our King, Shall through the heav'nly

trib - ute bring Hosanna! Ho-san-na! Ho-san-na to our Sav - ior King!
arch - es ring! Hosanna! Ho - san-na! Ho-san-nas ev - er to our King!

3. High we raise the strain,
   Loud it swells again,
   Moving onward—
   Ever onward
As the waves of ocean roll:
   And its burden—
   Precious burden!
Calms and soothes the weary soul!
   Chorus.

4. Oh! our blessed Lord,
   Now, with sweet accord,
   We before Thee,
   Do implore Thee
E'er to make these courts Thine own:
   Let Thy glory—
   Brightest glory!
Be in rich profusion shown. *Chorus.*

5. Come, thou risen King!
   Come, e'en while we sing:
   In life's morning,
   Life's adorning
Give us, while we seek Thy way;
   May we never
   From Thee sever,—
May we near Thee constant stay! *Chorus.*

6. Then, when life is o'er—
   Passed, the golden shore,
   O'er the River—
   Beauteous River!
Where the light of God doth shine,
   Songs resounding,
   Joys abounding,
E'er shall tell of Love divine ! *Chorus*

Work, for the Night is Coming.

From "Song Garden," (second book) by permission of Mason Brothers.

1. Work, for the night is com - ing, Work thro' the morn-ing hours;
2. Work, for the night is com - ing, Work thro' the sun - ny noon;
3. Work, for the night is com - ing, Un - der the sun - set skies;

Work while the dew is spark - ling, Work 'mid spring - ing flow'rs;
Fill bright - est hours with la - bor, Rest comes sure and soon.
While their bright tints are glow - ing, Work, for day - light flies.

Cres.

Work when the day grows bright - er, Work in the glow - ing sun;
Give eve - ry fly - ing min - ute Some-thing to keep in store;
Work till the last beam fad - eth, Fad - eth to shine no more;

Work, for the night is com - ing, When man's work is done.
Work, for the night is com - ing, When man works no more.
Work while the night is dark - 'ning, When man's work is done.

Responses to the Decalogue.

Lord have mercy upon us and incline our hearts to keep this law. A - men.

FINALE
Lord have mercy upon us and write all these thy laws upon our | hearts we be | seech thee.

Singing for Jesus.

"And he ministered with singing."

PHILLIPS.

1. Sing-ing for Je - sus, sing-ing for Je - sus, Try-ing to serve him wherever I go;

Point-ing the lost to the way of sal-va-tion—This be my mis-sion, a pil-grim be-low.

When in the strains of my country I mingle, When to exalt her my voice I would raise; 'Tis for his

glo-ry whose arm is her ref-uge, Him would I honor, his name would I praise,

His name would I praise.

2

Singing for Jesus glad hymns of devotion,
 Lifting the soul on her pinions of love;
Dropping a word or a thought by the wayside,
 Telling of rest in the mansions above.
Music may soften where language would fail us,
 Feelings long buried 'twill often restore,
Tones that were breathed from the lips of departed,
 How we revere them when they are no more

3.

Singing for Jesus, my blessed Redeemer,
 God of the pilgrims, for thee I will sing;
When o'er the billows of time I am wafted,
 Still with thy praise shall eternity ring.
Glory to God for the prospect before me,
 Soon shall my spirit transported ascend;
Singing for Jesus, O blissful employment,
 Loud hallelujahs that never will end.

Loved Ones Gone Before.

Words by Mrs. M. B. C. Slade.

Music by H. R. Palmer.

1. O'er the wa-ters, dark and foam-ing, Is a bright and peace-ful shore.
2. By the crys-tal streams of Heav-en, In its fields of fade-less flowers;
3. In the ma-ny-mansioned dwell-ing Of the ho-ly and the blest,

There the bliss-ful bands are roam-ing, Of our loved ones gone be-fore.
To our loved and lost are giv-en Pur-er joys than these of ours.
When the glad new song is swell-ing, Our be-lov-ed are at rest.

Just how near they stray to meet us, We can nev-er sure-ly know,
Do they whis-per, there the sto-ry Of their love for us be-low?
We will hush each sigh of sad-ness, Lest it reach that peace-ful land,

But their wel-com-ing will greet us When we launch our bark to go.
To those sum-mer hights of glo-ry, Do they long for us to go?
There will come an hour of glad-ness, We shall join the spir-it band.

Refrain.

We are com-ing, hap-py an-gels! O-pen wide the pear-ly gate;

Only just a lit-tle long-er Shall we la-bor, love, and wait,

We are com-ing hap-py an-gels! O-pen wide the pear-ly gate,

On-ly just a lit-tle long-er Shall we la-bor, love, and wait.

Let us Help Each Other.

Words by Dr. C. R. Blackall.　　　　　　　　　　　　　　　　H. R. Palmer.

1. Let us help each oth - er, o'er life's rug - ged way,
2. Let us help each oth - er, in the chris - tian way,
3. Let us help each oth - er, wea - ry is the way,
4. Let us help each oth - er, Je - sus makes the way,

Gent - ly lift the fall - en ones, re - claim - ing those who stray,
Taught by our Re - deem - er's life we can - not ev - er stray;
Dark the days and cheer - less, when from His dear path we stray;
Straight and ver - y pleas - ant when we do not choose to stray,

Cheer the sad and lone - ly, with our hap - py light,
Guid - ed by his coun - sel, look - ing toward the light,
Joy - ous - ly we hast - en toward the bless - ed light,
He will make the shad - ows dis - ap - pear in light,

Point the way of sure es - cape from death's dark night.
Which a - lone can save the lost from death's dark night.
Glad - ly turn our face a - way from death's dark night.
He will take a - way the gloom of death' dark night.

Let us Help Each Other. Concluded.

Refrain.

Let us help each oth - er, for there's much to do,

Let us help each oth - er, for there's much to do,

Striv - ing to be use - ful, pa - tient, kind, and true,

Striv - ing to be use - ful, pa - tient, kind, and true,

Eas - ing heav - y bur - dens oth - ers have to bear,

Eas - ing heav - y bur - dens oth - ers have to bear,

Let us e'er be rea - dy, joys and griefs to share.

Let us e'er be rea - dy, joys and griefs to share.

Jesus by the Sea.*

Reverentially.

GEO. F. ROOT.

1. O I love to think of Je - sus as he sat be - side the sea;
2. O I love to think of Je - sus as he walk'd up - on the sea;
3. O I love to think of Je - sus as he walk'd be - side the sea;

Where the waves were on - ly murm'ring on the strand; When he
When the waves were roll - ing fear - ful - ly and grand; How the
Where the fish - ers spread their nets up - on the shore; How he

sat with - in the boat, on the sil - ver waves a - float,
winds and waves were still, at the bid - ding of his will,
bade them fol - low him, and for - sake the paths of sin,

While he taught the wait - ing peo - ple on the land.
While he brought his lov'd dis - ci - ples safe to land.
And to be his true dis - ci - ples ev - er - more.

*From Chapel Gems, by Permission of Root & Cady

Refrain.

O I love to think of Je - sus by the sea;
O I love to think of Je - sus by the sea;
O I love to think of Je - sus by the sea;

O I love to think of Je - sus by the sea, And I
O I love to think of Je - sus by the sea, How he
O I love to think of Je - sus by the sea, And I

love the pre · cious Word, Which he spake to them that heard,
walk'd u - pon the wave, His be - lov - ed ones to save,
long to leave my all, At the dear Re - deem - er's call,

While he taught the wait - ing peo - ple by the sea.
While he brought them safe - ly o'er the storm - y sea.
And his true dis - ci - ple ev - er - more to be.

Who are these in bright array.

Soprano Solo. By H. R. Palmer.

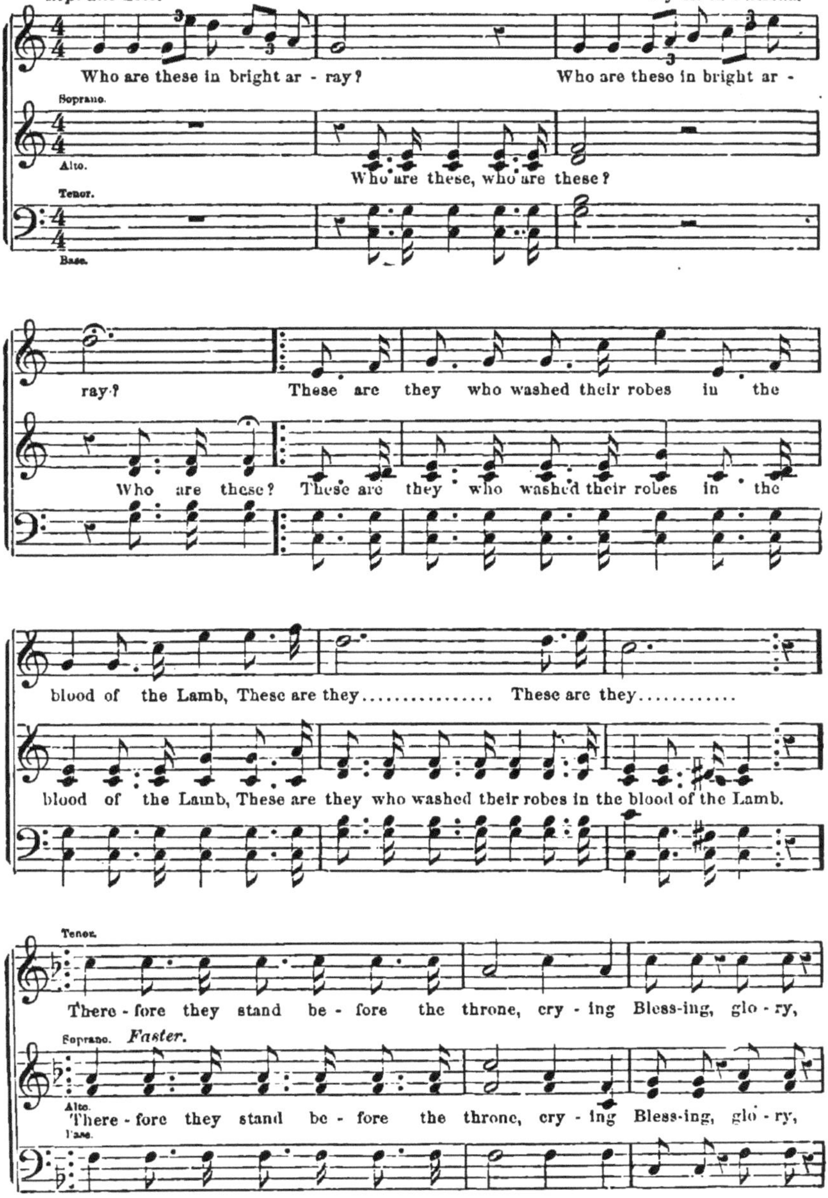

wis - dom,   hon - or,   Pow - er and might be un - to   God, ev - er,

wis - dom, hon - or,   Pow - er and might be un - to   God, ev - er,

A TEMPO.

world with-out   end.   They shall   hun - ger no more, Neither
                              They shall   walk by the streams of the

world with-out   end.   They shall   hun - ger no more, Neither
                              They shall   walk by the streams of the

thirst   a - ny more, For the   Lamb up - on the throne shall feed them:
foun - tain of life, For the   Lamb up - on the throne shall lead them:

thirst   a - ny more, For the   Lamb up - on the throne shall feed them:
foun - tain of life, For the   Lamb up - on the throne shall lead them.

REPEAT PP.

For   the   Lamb up - on the throne shall   lead them,
For   the   Lamb up - on the throne shall....(OMIT.)........ lead them.

For   the   Lamb up - on the throne shall   lead them,
For   the   Lamb up - on the throne shall....(OMIT)........ lead them.

From the Recesses of a lowly Spirit.

A - men.

1. From the recesses of a lowly spirit
   Our humble prayer ascends; O | Father, | hear it;—
   Borne on the trembling wings of fear and meekness;
   Forgive its | weakness.

2. We know, we feel, how mean and how unworthy
   The lowly sacrifice we | pour be- | fore thee:
   What can we offer thee, O thou most holy!
   But | sin and | folly!

3. We see thy hand—it leads us, it supports us;—
   We hear thy voice—it | counsels,...and it | courts us;
   And then we turn away!—yet still thy kindness
   For- | gives our | blindness.

4. Who can resist thy gentle call, appealing
   To every generous thought and | grateful | feeling?—
   O, who can hear the accents of thy mercy,
   And | never | love thee?

5. Kind Benefactor ! plant within this bosom
   The | seeds of | holiness, | and let them blossom
   In fragrance, and in beauty bright and vernal
   And | spring e- | ternal.

6. Then place them in those everlasting gardens
   Where angels walk, and | seraphs....are the | wardens;—
   Where every flower—brought safe through death's dark portal—
   Be | comes im- | mortal.

O Give Thanks.

CONTRIBUTED.

Solo or Quartette.   Chorus of Teacher and Scholars.

1. O give thanks unto the Lord for he is good: For his mer-cy en-dur-eth for - ev - er.

O give thanks unto the God of gods! For his mer-cy en-dur-eth for - ev - er.   A-men.

3. O give thanks unto the Lord of lords;   *Cho.* For his mercy, &c.
4. To him who alone doeth great wonders;   *Cho.* For his mercy, &c.
5. To him that by wisdom made the heavens;   *Cho.* For his mercy, &c.
6. To him that stretched out the earth above the waters; *Cho.* For his mercy, &c.
7. To him that made great lights;   *Cho.* For his mercy, &c.
8. The sun to rule by day; the moon and stars to rule by night; *Cho.* For his, &c.
9. Who remembered us in our low estate;   *Cho.* For his mercy, &c.
10. And hath redeemed us from our enemies;   *Cho.* For his mercy, &c.
11. Who giveth food to all flesh;   *Cho.* For his mercy, &c.
12. O give thanks unto thee God of heaven;   *Cho.* For his mercy, &c.

The Savior's Call.

Words by Dr. C. R. Blackall.

G. C. Pearson.

1. The Sav - ior stands in - vit - ing, His arms are o - pen wide,
2. In love he doth im - plore us . To turn a - side, and live;
3. Shall Love be spurned, thus proffered, And cast a - way as nought,—
4. Oh, no! we'll heed it ev - er, He shall not plead in vain,

He calls us from our slight - ing, As those for whom he died.
He deep - ly yearn - eth o'er us, Though noth - ing we can give.
Shall bless - ing free - ly of - fered, By us be worth - less thought?
We will be His for - ev - er, And with him we shall reign.

Refrain.

Come, oh! come, 'tis Je - sus' voice, Call - ing us from sin a - way,

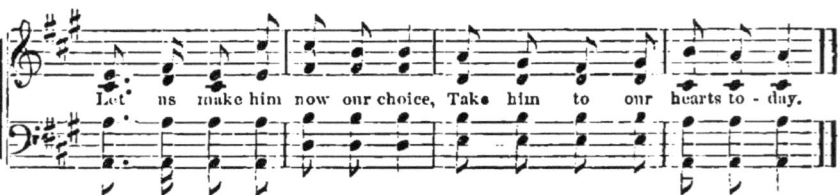

Let us make him now our choice, Take him to our hearts to - day.

Doxology.

H. R. Palmer.

1st. time.

2d. time.

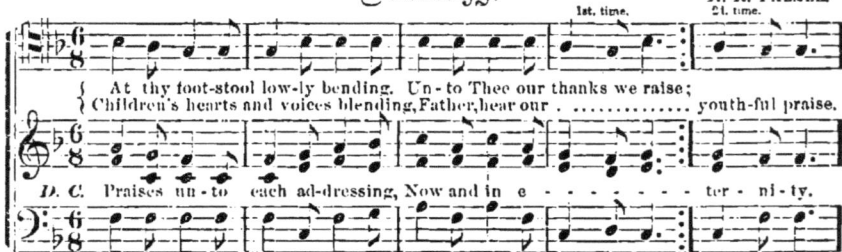

{ At thy foot-stool low-ly bending. Un - to Thee our thanks we raise;
{ Children's hearts and voices blending, Father, hear our .... youth-ful praise.

D. C. Praises un - to each ad-dressing, Now and in e - - - - - - - ter - ni - ty.

D. C.

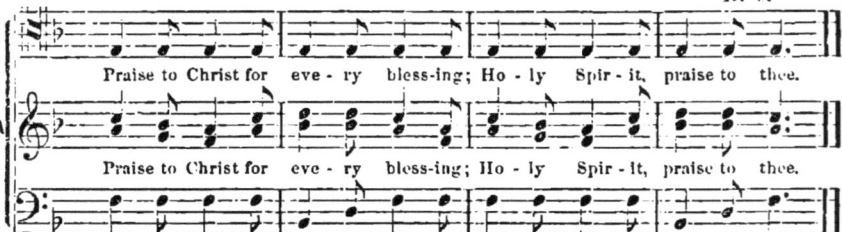

Praise to Christ for eve - ry bless-ing; Ho - ly Spir - it, praise to thee.

Praise to Christ for eve - ry bless-ing; Ho - ly Spir - it, praise to thee.

INDEX.

www.ingramcontent.com/pod-product-compliance
Lightning Source LLC
Chambersburg PA
CBHW032358280326
41935CB00008B/617